Dwight Lyman Moody

Ten Days with D. L. Moody

Comprising a Collection of His Sermons, also Sermons and Addresses by Prominent Christian workers at the Christian Convention held at Northfield, Mass.

Dwight Lyman Moody

Ten Days with D. L. Moody
Comprising a Collection of His Sermons, also Sermons and Addresses by Prominent Christian workers at the Christian Convention held at Northfield, Mass.

ISBN/EAN: 9783337160890

Printed in Europe, USA, Canada, Australia, Japan

Cover: Foto ©Lupo / pixelio.de

More available books at **www.hansebooks.com**

D. L. MOODY,

Comprising a Collection of

His Sermons,

Also Sermons and Addresses by prominent Christian workers at the Christian Convention held at Northfield, Mass., the home of Mr. Moody.

Reported for The New York Weekly Witness, and Published by Arrangement with John Dougall & Co.

THE SERMON SERIES, No. 3.

Issued Monthly.   Subscription, $3.00 per year.   November, 1886.
Entered at New York Post office as second-class matter.

NEW YORK:
J. S. OGILVIE AND COMPANY,
31 Rose Street.

Copyright, 1886, by
J. S. OGILIVIE AND COMPANY.

TEN DAYS WITH MR. MOODY.

NORTHFIELD, THE HOME OF MR. MOODY.

Northfeld is perhaps as near an approach to Heaven on earth as can anywhere be found. While driving along the main street from the station you admire the tall spreading elms which line the wide avenue. But when you reach the north end of the town and approach Mr. Moody's house, a scene bursts upon the view to which I know no parallel. In the foreground, looking west, the vari-colored fields slope down to the Connecticut river, which supplies to the picture the element of water, and can be seen for many miles of its course. Beyond the river, very gradually and gently rises a range of verdure-clad hills extending as far as the eye can reach in both directions, and toward the north over-topped in the dim distance by bluish mountain peaks. From the seminary buildings the panorama is somewhat modified, but in its general aspects much the same. The whole effect is that of serenity and repose.— The voice of Nature is the voice of peace. The place is hallowed by its later uses; and in a word, it is a morsel of Paradise regained.

Mr. Moody looks as hale and ruddy as ever. His

physical resources are apparently unbounded, and his spiritual power waxes greater as the years go on. He is of course the dominating genius of these institutions, and in everything one can see the impress of his keenly practical mind, as well as of his rare attainments in the higher nature. The value of the example of a living personal embodiment of real Christianity is seen in the admirable daily life of the pupils of the schools, many of whom are just now employed in various capacities in attending to the wants of the visitors. The moral atmosphere is sunny; all seem happy; and in their work they seem eager to help one another, and to anticipate the slightest wish of every guest.

MOODY'S SCHOOLS.

If Mr. Moody had done nothing else than to found these schools, and establish the type of Christian living which here prevails—sending forth multitudes of young men and maidens fully equipped unto every good work—he would have achieved a result with which most men would rest content. A little incident will illustrate his rough-and-ready application of common sense: Said he, walking across the grounds the other evening, "Do you see that line of posts up on that hill, where the horses are tied? Well, there are some boys who want to come here, and I said to them yesterday, 'Do you think you could go and get some posts, and plant them in the ground, to tie the horses to? If you don't, I don't want you.' They thought they could, and that's what they have done since yesterday. They had to go and find the posts themselves, put them in the ground, and board them together." With such kindly, but discriminating treatment, it is no wonder his pupils are all self-reliant, docile and diligent.

SANKEY SOUND YET.

Mr. Sankey, I am happy to say, has not looked better for years. He tells me the reports of his illness in London were much exaggerated. He had an attack of liver complaint as a result of seven months of overwork; but the rumors as to his loss of voice were groundless. "Now," he says, "I have got back my liver, and I am all right." Certainly I have not heard him sing better within recent recollection. His voice is clear, melodious and powerful, and the peculiar pathos and charm of expression which place him easily alone among singers, have fully reappeared. Now that Mr. Moody has called to his aid a newer man in the department of song, Mr. Sankey is not likely to be so hard-worked, and will, it is to be hoped, be better able to preserve his health. He has taken a house in Northfield, and the Divine favor evidently rests upon him richly in every way.

THE NEW SINGER.

Considerable curiosity has been evinced to see and hear Mr. Moody's new singer, Mr. Towner, and it is the unanimous verdict that he has secured a prize. All are greatly pleased with the new acquisition, both as a singer and as a man. Mr. Towner was born in North-eastern Pennsylvania, in the same region which gave to the world Mr Bliss and Mr. McGranahan. His father was a noted singer and choir organizer, and was the first instructor of P. P. Bliss. He himself began life as a local teacher and leader of musical institutes. His first appearance in a wider field was as the singing companion of Dr. L. W. Munhall, recently Y. M. C. A. State Secretary of Indiana, and now an evangelist. Dr. Munhall was the organizer of Mr. Moody's tour in the western States last Winter, and thus Moody was brought into contact with Towner. He has secured him at a comfortable salary for a term of five years. Mr. Towner's manner of singing is like, and yet unlike, that of other singing evangelists. "Shut your eyes," says Mr. Moody, "and you would think you were hearing Bliss." I have heard Mr. Bliss, and while there is a resemblance in some respects, in others there is a great resemblance to Mr. Sankey. Mr. Towner is taller than either Moody or Sankey, is of slender build and young-looking, with bright eyes, thin mustache, and no beard. His voice is a clear strong baritone, in good cultivation, and with a distinct enunciation like Mr. Sankey's, and a speaking rather than singing manner which is very effective. He excels as an organizer and trainer of choirs, and composes music of high merit. A hardy physique renders him available for the extremely trying work in which Mr. Moody has lately been engaged. "Last Winter," said he, "we were on an average two nights a week on the rail, and at every place we went to I had to deal with new material and lead the singing almost alone. The strain was terrible. So they say I am about the only man Mr Moody can't lay on his back."

GREAT IMPROVEMENTS.

Those who were here in 1881 are surprised to see the many changes and improvements. Two new buildings have risen, as if by magic, on the grounds of the Girls' Seminary, and another in connection with the Boys' School at Mount Hermon. The oldest building, now called East Hall, it will be remembered, is situated some distance from the road up the hill on the northern side of Mr. Moody's house. Farther north, nearer the road, and on the edge of the Bonar Glen, there has been erected a larger and very handsome building, called Marquand Hall. It cost sixty thousand dollars, which came from the Marquand estate, of which Mr. D. W. McWilliams, of Brooklyn, is residuary legatee. Work was begun last summer, and the opening took place in January of this year. The material is dark red brick. The style is a modification of the Queen Anne, with the close-cut eaves, low ceilings and small-paned windows of that order, combined with many modern features. The building is used entirely as a dormitory, and is capable of accommodating eighty students, with office, drawing-room, dining-hall, chapel, etc. On the fifth of February occurred the birthday of Mr. Moody's mother, and a reception was held in this building. Mr. Moody's forty-eighth birthday was the same day, but the celebration was chiefly in honor of "Grandma Moody." The loving hands of the pupils placed over the large fireplace in the chapel the inscription, which still remains: "Her children arise up and call her blessed." Telegrams of congratulation were received from all over the world. There are now three dormitories connected with the seminary, with a combined scholarship of one hundred and eighty, namely, sixty in the East Hall, eighty in the Marquand Hall, and forty in a reconstructed farmhouse by the roadside, called Bonar Hall. About midway between Marquand Hall and East Hall stands a handsome new building of granite, used as a recitation hall. No name has yet been given to it, but because of the material, it is generally called Stone Hall. The cost of this building, like the new building at Mount Hermon, was borne by the hymn-book fund. Mr. Moody says, when pointing to either structure: "Mr. Sankey sang that building up." Stone Hall is a very massive-looking two-story and basement building. The first story is divided into class-rooms. In designing the second story, the first thought was to use it for recitation rooms; but Mr. Moody concluded that he must have some place for congregational purposes, so that this hall is now used as the principal auditorium. The recitation halls on the first floor are sufficient at present, but if more are needed, it is designed to add wings to the building, which will also afford room for a library. This hall was dedicated on the seventeenth of June. Much care and labor have been expended in beautifying the grounds, so that they now present the aspect of a park. A winding, macadamized drive, takes the place of the straight earth road in front of East Hall, and similar drives afford access to the other buildings. Foot-walks will be added later.

THE GATHERING.

Dr. Pentecost, of Brooklyn, who has a summer residence here, Dr. Pierson, of Philadelphia, and Dr. Gordon, of Boston, are among the distinguished speakers in attendance. Pastors, evangelists, superintendents of city missions, and Christian workers of every kind, to the number of about five hundred, are on the ground, thronging the meetings, exchanging thoughts, hints for work, and discoveries in the deep thoughts of Scripture.

DR. PIERSON'S ADDRESS.

At the opening meeting on Wednesday forenoon, August 5, the principal speaker was the Rev. Dr. Arthur T. Pierson, pastor of the Bethany Presbyterian Church (connected with John Wannamaker's famous Sunday-school) in Philadelphia. His subject was, "Being filled with the Spirit." In Ephesians v, 18, Paul says: "Be not drunk with wine, wherein is excess; but be filled with the Spirit." Evidently he had in mind a contrast between the sensual effects of strong drink and that Divine intoxication which comes from being filled with the Holy Spirit. What are the effects of alcoholic inebriation? An expansion of vision followed by blurring of sight; unnatural exhibitions before the brain, great hilarity, followed by moroseness; on the muscular system, in stimulating to efforts; upon the speech, in muddling language. How different the effects of the Holy Spirit? What are they? The eyes see with truth and power; the mind is aroused to grand efforts of thought; the faculty of speech to most gracious and eloquent utterances; while the whole person is strengthened and the disposition attuned to the spirit of Christ. The effects of drink in excess are disastrous; no man can ever be filled with the Holy Ghost to excess. We need to realize more the personality of the Holy Ghost. A Brooklyn clergyman lately defined the Holy Spirit as a shadowy effluence proceeding from the Father and the Son. How would it sound if he should baptize a child "in the name of the Father, and of the Son, and of the shadowy effluence," etc. Deny the personality of the Holy Ghost and you deny everything. The fullness of the Holy Ghost would be an eye-salve on the ministers of the land, so much clearer would they see. How are we to arrive at this fullness of the Spirit? The twenty-ninth chapter of Exodus tells us. If we, by putting ourselves aloof from our sins and unclean things, hallow ourselves to the utmost, the Holy Spirit will enter us fully, and Himself sanctify us.

DR. PENTECOST'S ADDRESS.

In the afternoon, the Rev. Dr. Pentecost, of Brooklyn, took for a subject: "The sin and the danger of offering strange fire in our service of the Lord." Satan, he said, had been busy not only filling the world with sin, but defiling whatever is good. He counterfeits the best things God has done for men. The Lord Himself finds him in his own wheat-field oversowing the wheat with tares. We are not ignorant of his devices, and it will be well for us to look closely into the most holy things, and see whether they are really of God or of some other spirit. In Leviticus X. we read how Nadab and Abihu offered strange fire before the Lord, and were smote with fire that they died. They were the sons of Aaron. This was the very beginning of the Mosaic dispensation. The whole circumstance was startling, and it ought to startle us. Notice that fire is spoken of throughout the Bible as a symbol of the presence of God and His energy. Thus it appeared in the flaming sword at the Garden of Eden, in the burning bush, in the pillar of cloud and fire, in the great Shekinah of the Temple, and in the altar sacrifices. With fire Elijah fought out his great battle with the priests of Baal. In the New Testament the gift of the Holy Ghost was made manifest to the people in tongues of fire. The service of the Israelites was very similar to that of surrounding nations; but whereas the latter kindled the fires upon their altars, God distinguished His service by sending down fire from Heaven. That is the difference between true religion and its counterfeit. Natural religion depends on the energy of the flesh. Supernatural religion depends on the energy of the Spirit of God, which comes down from above. It is quite possible to be perfectly right in the forms of our service, and yet destitute of Divine power. To see how essential is this fire from above, look out two or three passages. In Genesis iv, 4, God had respect to Abel's offering, and hence He must have burnt it with fire. In Judges vi, 21, when Gideon had laid the flesh and cakes upon the rock, the angel touched them and they were consumed by fire. No doubt the messenger had looked like an ordinary man, but now Gideon perceived that he was the angel of the Lord. On Mount Carmel the priests of Baal might have kindled a fire, but it would not have been heavenly fire. It was the fire from Heaven which vindicated Elijah and attested the true God. In I Chronicles xxi. 26, David made an offering, and called upon the Lord; and He answered him from heaven by fire. In II Chronicles, vii. 1, when Solomon had made an end of praying, the fire came down from Heaven, and the glory of the Lord filled the house. Fire, then, we see, is the symbol of the Holy Ghost. In the New Testament this is still more clear. The Divine energy, as finally manifested to the Church, was in the form of tongues of fire. But beware of strange fire! In Leviticus xvi, 12, Aaron was bidden to take a censer of live coals from off the altar of the Lord, and use it to offer up incense. He must not kindle the censer with any other fire but that which had come down from Heaven. It was the neglect and contempt of this commandment which constituted the sin of Nadab and Abihu. They dared to worship God with strange fire. Suppose the Apostles who had been told to tarry at Jerusalem till fire was sent down from Heaven had dared to disobey. Suppose Peter had said to John, "John, four or five days have passed, and how do we know the Spirit is coming? Perhaps it has come. We know the Gospel; we are witnesses of the crucifixion and the resurrection. Why not go and preach?" What would have happened? The message would have been an utter failure. We have the Gospel, we have the right forms, but oh! let us beware of preaching in the energy of the flesh. We must have Holy Ghost power. Nadab and Abihu were slain at the very beginning of the Mosaic dispensation. Ananias and Sapphira were struck dead at the very beginning of the history of the Church. The speaker said he sometimes trembled lest a strange fire had crept unawares into his own service. We need to watch.

Rev. R. C. Morse, secretary of the International Committee Y. M. C. A., spoke for ten minutes on "What more can be done to reach our young men." He described the vast work accomplished by the Young Men's Christian Association, and showed the need of multiplying the workers in this fruitful vineyard.

MR. MOODY'S ADDRESS ON THE BIBLE.

At the forenoon meeting of Thursday Mr. Moody spoke on "The Bible: how to study it, and how to use it." He said, in substance: It is a great thing to acquire, an appetite for the Word of God. If we can get a love for the Word, we will get something that will last. I would like to find the first Christian feeding upon the Word of God without growing. A great many Christians wonder why they don't grow. It's because they are not feeding. A good many souls are all dried up, all withered up, because they haven't been fed. I think David had this idea when he wrote the one hundred and nineteenth Psalm. There must be something in the fact that the longest chapter in the Bible is about the Bible itself. I want to call your attention to nine passages in the one hundred and nineteenth Psalm: twenty-fifth verse—"Quicken me according to Thy Word." Thirty-seventh verse—"Quicken Thou me in Thy way." Fortieth verse—"Quicken me in Thy righteousness." What does this nation need to-day more than to be quickened in righteousness? It is not mere gush and sentiment this nation wants, so much as it is a revival of downright honesty. Fiftieth verse—"This is my comfort in my affliction: for Thy Word hath quickened me." 88th verse—

"Quicken me with Thy loving kindness." Ninety-third verse—"I will never forget Thy precepts, for with them Thou hast quickened me." One hundred and seventh verse—"I am afflicted very much: quicken me, O Lord, according to Thy Word." One hundred and fifty-sixth verse—"Plead my cause and deliver me; quicken me according to Thy Word." One hundred and fifty-sixth verse—"Great are Thy tender mercies, O Lord; quicken me according to Thy judgments." That is the way it goes—quicken me according to Thy Word, according to Thy precepts, according to Thy way. That's what we all want to pray this morning. An old Scotchman made this remark: "David said 'I have hid Thy Word in my heart.' That was a good thing, in a good place, for a good purpose." Some people carry the Bible under their arms. Well, that's better than not to carry it at all. Some people have got a good deal of it in their heads. That's better. But when you get it in the heart, that is best of all. When a man gets the Bible in his heart, it is going to make a change in his whole life. The trouble with a good many Christians is they are good in spots. A man once said he had a good well, only it would dry up in Summer and freeze up in Winter. Some Christians are just like that well—good at certain times. But when a man is feeding on the Word of God he is good all the time. I really think that instead of so many of the prayer-meetings we have, we ought to have more meetings for reading and studying the Word of God. When I pray, I am talking to God; when I am reading the Word, it is God speaking to me. David said the Word of God was like fire in his bones. I don't believe a man or woman is fit for God's service till they catch fire in this way.

THE NEW TESTAMENT AND THE OLD.

Now, it is getting to be very common—very fashionable in certain quarters, even among professed Christians—to hear men say, "I believe in the New Testament, but I don't believe in the Old." We hear that on the right hand and on the left. I pray to God that we may be delivered from this idea. It is doing a thousand times more harm than all the lectures of infidels to hear Christians say, "This and this isn't inspired." One minister said he had cut everything down to the four Gospels. They contained everything, and he didn't see why he shouldn't do as St. Paul did, and go to the fountain head. It wasn't long before that man fell into sin. Unsound in doctrine, unsound in practice. We want to believe the whole Bible. We want to take the whole of it, from Genesis to Revelation. It is most absurd to hear a man talk about believing the New Testament, and not believing the Old. In the four Gospels Christ quotes from twenty-two of the books of the Old Testament. I suppose we get only a fragment of what Christ said. I believe that for years after the death of Christ the air was full of the words which fell from His lips. And, so, I have no doubt, that in His quotations from the Old Testament He quoted from every book. In His words, as recorded in Matthew, we find nineteen quotations, in Mark fifteen, in Luke twenty-five, and in John eleven different passages; not only just isolated verses, but great blocks taken out of the Old Testament and transferred into the New. So you see how absurd it is for men to say they believe in the New and don't believe in the Old. Why, the New Testament is made up largely from passages from the Old. Over and over again you will hear Christ say, "This is done that the Scriptures might be fulfilled." In Hebrews there are eighty-five Old Testament quotations. In Revelation there are two hundred and forty-five—more than in any other book. "Heaven and earth shall pass away," said Christ, "but My word shall not pass away." How absurd for any one to think the Word of God is going to pass away! There never was a time in the history of the world when so many Bibles were being printed as there are to-day. When Christ was speaking those words I can just imagine I hear some infidel saying: "'Heaven and earth shall pass away, but My word shall not pass away!' Hear that Jewish peasant talk! I never heard such conceit in my life from any one." There was no shorthand reporter taking down His words, and they seemed to have been lost. But nearly nineteen hundred years pass away, and His words are going to the very corners of the earth, in two hundred and fifty different languages. There are about 1,400,000,000 people in the world, and over 200,000,000 copies of the Bible have been printed by the American Bible Society and the British and Foreign Bible Society. Then there are societies in Germany, France, and other countries, exclusive of individuals, that are printing and circulating the

Scriptures. In fact, there have been more Bibles printed in the last seventy years than there were in the previous eighteen hundred years. I consider that a greater miracle than any other which Christ wrought when He was here on earth. I'm glad I live in the present day and can see it.

WHAT MEN CAVIL AT.

A lady said to me lately, "I can't believe that Elijah was fed by ravens. Do you?" I have no more doubt that the ravens fed Elijah than I have that I stand here. The very things in the Old Testament that men cavil at the most to-day are the things the Son of Man set His seal to when He was down here, and it is not good policy for a servant to be above his master. The Master believed these things. Some one says: "You don't believe the story of Noah and the flood, do you?" Yes; I believe that as much as I believe the Sermon on the Mount. Christ said that when He should come again it would be as in the days of Noah, when men were eating and drinking, and the flood came and took them all off. "You don't believe Lot's wife was turned into a pillar of salt!" Yes: Christ said: "As it was in the days of Lot, so shall it be in the coming of the Son of Man." *He* believed that story of Lot's wife—hadn't any doubt about it. "Do you believe that the children of Israel were fed in the desert on manna?" Christ said: "Your fathers ate manna." "Do you believe the Israelites were saved by looking on a brass serpent?" Christ said: "Even as Moses lifted up the brazen serpent." Men will stretch their necks, and look very wise, and say: "Why, you don't believe that story about Jonah and the whale?" Yes, I do. Christ said: "For as Jonah was three days in the whale's belly, so shall the Son of Man be three days in the bowels of the earth." "But," they say, "this was impossible. The whale is so constructed that it couldn't swallow a man." Well; what does the Bible say? "God prepared a great fish." If He could speak this world into existence, I think He could speak a fish into existence big enough to swallow a man. I have a good deal of sympathy with that old colored woman who said if the Bible said Jonah swallowed the whale she would believe it; God could make a man large enough to swallow a whale. There's no trouble about these things, dear friends; no difficulty at all. One of these modern philosophers, discussing the story of Balaam, said he had examined the mouth of an ass, and it was physically impossible for an ass to speak. "Ah," said a friend; "you make an ass, and I will make him speak." There's nothing more unreasonable than infidelity.

THE BEST WAY TO CONVERT INFIDELS.

The best way to convert an infidel is to take him to the prophecies fulfilled. Look at the prophecies concerning Christ. "His name shall be called wonderful." Wasn't everything about Him wonderful? born of a virgin, carried into Egypt, astounding the doctors when twelve years old in the Temple. Everything about His three years' ministry was wonderful—the miracles He performed, His crucifixion with the sun darkened and the vail of the Temple rent, His resurrection. Isn't His name wonderful to-day. Nineteen hundred years have passed, and what crowds will flock to hear about Christ! No other name could have brought you into this little town. Nothing else brought you from all over the country but to be with Jesus. Yes; His name is called wonderful.

A BLESSING IN THE PROPHECIES.

And so, my friends, what we want is just to take up the Word of God and let it speak for itself. I have been wonderfully blessed to-day in reading about Babylon falling. Take the prophecies in regard to Ninevah, and see how they have been fulfilled. When I was in the British Museum, a lady called my attention to certain relics from Ninevah. I looked at them with more interest through her specs. In Nahum iii, 6, the Lord says concerning Ninevah: "I will cast abominable filth upon thee, and make thee vile, and will set thee as a gazing stock." Isn't that exactly what it is, with hundreds of thousands of people looking at these things in the British Museum taken up out of Ninevah. "They that look upon thee shall flee from thee, and say, Ninevah is laid waste." Isn't it what travelers are saying to-day? And then look at Tyre. In Ezekiel xxvi, 5, the Lord says: "It shall be a place for the spreading of nets in the middle of the sea." Mr. Corbin, correspondent of the Boston *Journal*, visited Palestine in 1868, and he has told me that one night, pitching his tent on the side of Tyre, what should he see but a number of men on a bare rock spreading their fishing nets. Taking out his Bible he read this prophecy, and noticed how literally it was fulfilled.

THINGS WE DON'T UNDERSTAND.

It is true there are things in the Bible we don't understand, but we are not going to say, "I don't believe it because I don't understand it." A man said to me once, "What do you do with that passage? How do you understand it?" "I don't understand it." "How do you explain it?" "I don't explain it." "What do you do?" "I don't do anything." There are lots of things I believe that I don't understand. There are a good many things in astronomy, a good many things about my own system, I don't understand; yet I believe them. And I'm glad there *are* things in the Bible I don't understand. If I could take that book up and read it as I would any other book, I might think I could write a book like that, and so could you. I am glad there are heights I haven't been able to climb up to. I am glad there are depths I haven't been able to fathom. It's the best proof that the book came from God. I suppose there are a good many things in the prophecies concerning Christ that no one could understand till Christ came and fulfilled them. Just look at some of those prophecies. He was to be born in Bethlehem, and carried into Egypt. When that announcement was made, how strange it must have sounded! But when the time came, God put the whole world in motion to bring Mary to Bethlehem, so that Jesus might be born there. Cæsar issued a decree that the whole world should be taxed. All this was done just to bring that virgin up to Bethlehem. I believe that God would have created a world rather than that any prophecy should be unfulfilled.

ECCLESIASTICAL SPOONS.

Now the question is, How are you going to read this book? When I was a young man I thought I must be fed with ecclesiastical spoons. Sometimes I got sawdust; sometimes I got salt; sometimes I got bread. When my little boy Paul first learned to find the way to his mouth, he wanted everybody to know about it, and it was a great event in our family. Lots of men have been in the Church forty years, and if you ask them what they believe they will say, "What the Church believes." "Well, what does the Church believe?" "I don't know." I don't believe any child of God is going to grow till he has learned to feed himself. What may be good for me may not be good for you.

ONE BOOK AT A TIME.

I have been wonderfully blessed, in studying the Bible, by taking up one book at a time. I used to try to read the Bible through in a year. I would as soon read a dictionary that way now. Sometimes I want something to stir me up; other days, I want something to comfort me. When you read right through, you don't get much comfort. It is a great deal better, it seems to me, to take a book at a time. Or take a character. Or take a type. How many antetypes there were of Christ—Adam, Abel, Enoch, Abraham, Isaac, Jacob, Joseph, and so on all through the Old Testament. What a beautiful type Joseph is—hated, rejected, and then raised to a throne. You can't look into these things without getting fed. Another good thing is to take a subject. That's what we are trying to do in the Boy's School—and that's how we are getting the boy's grounded in the fundamental doctrines of the Bible. Take "Repentance," for example. Read up everything you can find about repentance. Take time. Suppose you spend a month; you couldn't spend it better. Get people's idea of repentance, and then see what the Bible says about it. Dozens of people have repented who don't know what repentance is. They think they have got to have some strange kind of feeling. A man I used to meet up here in Vermont would say to me every time I spoke to him, "Mr. Moody, it hasn't struck me yet. A neighbor of mine has been converted, and he has been a changed man since; but it hasn't struck me." Lots of people think repentance is going to strike them like lightning. Well, now, repentance don't come in that way. See what Bible repentance is. It isn't fear, it isn't feeling. Then take up "Conversion." Lots of people say, "I hate that word." In some churches there isn't much said about it, because people don't like it. But I have learned that sometimes the medicine people don't like, may be the very best medicine for them. I don't like to take pills, but they may be the very thing I need. When people shrug their shoulders and say, "I don't like conversion," it is just the thing they want.

REGENERATION.

Take up the Scripture doctrine of the necessity of being born again. Lots of people think they can go to Heaven on a good moral character. Look at the parable of the Prodigal Son. I would rather be the younger brother than the other. The elder brother had what the world calls a good moral character, and yet I think he was about the meanest case in the whole Bible. He wouldn't rejoice when his younger brother got home, and didn't like it when his father had mercy on him. What caused joy in the father's heart caused envy in his. When he heard music and dancing he wouldn't go in, and just marred that beautiful scene. Many churches are in the position of that elder brother, and don't believe in conversion. I wonder what some of these people will do when they get to Heaven, and some converted thief is brought in. I suppose they'll say, "Don't come near me. I don't want to be near you." Or when they meet Mary Magdalene, what will they do? I just think they will have to have a little corner in Heaven somewhere off by themselves. They can't sing the song of Moses and the Lamb—the song of redemption. A man must be made meet for the Kingdom of God before he will want to go there. Put a man in the presence of God before he is made meet for that presence, and he won't want to stay—it would be hell there for him. A man must be born of the Spirit—born again—regenerated.

We are hearing a good deal about reform, but what we want is regeneration. Then take up "Faith." We have got false ideas about faith.

FAITH.

I used to think that God was going to give me all the faith I wanted right away. I was going to do wonders. God was going to give me faith enough to remove mountains—turn the world upside down. "Faith cometh by knowledge." The more you know about people the more faith you will have in them, if they deserve it. You will have faith in a good man if you have known him two years; but you will know him a good deal better after ten years, and you will have more faith in him. Faith grows. And the way to get acquainted with God is by studying His Word.

PARDON AND JUSTIFICATION.

Take up "Justification" and "Pardon." Lots of people don't know there is any difference between the two things. But there is a great deal of difference. Suppose I commit some crime, and I am convicted, and then the Governor pardons me. I come back to this town a pardoned man. But suppose the judge says there is nothing against me; I come back in a different position. There is a good deal of difference between justification and pardon. What you want is to read up these subjects. It is a great thing to be a justified man—God-justified. And I think that brings light upon that eighth chapter of Romans. Who shall condemn one of God's elect? God justified me, and is he going to let anyone turn round and bring something against me? That would be a queer God, wouldn't it—a queer judge? These great doctrines ought to be studied. Take "Sanctification." I hear a great many people talking about sanctification; but I think we ought to go more to the Bible to see what it says, and let the Word of God speak for itself. When I was converted I thought I was going to have no more trouble with the old nature. But I soon found that the old nature was there. I had just as bad a temper as if I hadn't been converted, and I would say, "Why, that is the old temper coming back." By-and-by I learned that when a man is converted he has got two natures, the carnal nature and the spiritual nature. He has got a higher nature and a lower nature. He has got the old man yet. Do you think he is dead? Judicially he is, but in reality he ain't. If he was, you wouldn't have to watch him, would you? If a man is dead he ain't going to run away, is he? We have to keep watching the old man, and putting him in subjection all the time. I don't know any doctrine that needs more to be preached in our churches than this, that there is danger of the old man coming back. I haven't got time to speak of the doctrine of the Resurrection. I've got more comfort out of that doctrine than any other in the whole Bible. I look forward to the time when I am going to have a resurrected body. My Saviour is going to give me a body like His glorious body, that cannot faint and cannot die. It is going to be just like His. I don't know anything that will take a man out of the world much quicker than this idea. You must look in the New York papers to see how bonds and stocks are. It takes a man right out of the current of the world. Then there is the controversy about the Millennium. Some say Christ is coming at the beginning of the thousand years, and others that He is coming at the end of it. Let the Bible speak for itself. Don't listen to what this man and that man says about it, but study the Bible. And as Bishop Stevens, of Philadelphia, used to say, "Don't study it with your little red light of Methodism, or your little blue light of Presbyterianism, or the light of the Episcopal Church, but just the light of Calvary." Come without prejudice and say, "Whatever this book teaches I must receive." Don't say, "Well, I don't believe He is coming anyway for a thousand years." Take up the doctrine of "Assurance."

ASSURANCE.

A good many people honestly believe that it is presumptuous to say they are saved—that they have passed from death unto life—that they are going to have a place at God's right hand. But this book teaches very clearly that we can know we are saved. If we want light we can get it. We can know we have passed from death unto life if we are in earnest about it. There are twenty-one chapters in the Gospel of John, and they all speak of believing. "Believe" is the key of that Gospel. It just runs right straight on in the whole book. But turn over into John's first Epistle, and you will find that the key to that Epistle is "Know." Forty-two times that word occurs in these few chapters. "These things are written that ye might know." I don't believe it is the mind of God we should go through the world in darkness, not knowing whether we have been saved or not. I think the best book on Assurance is the first Epistle of John. If you are in doubt about your own salvation, read it, and you will know. I think Christ taught this doctrine very clearly when the disciples came back to Him after He had sent them out by twos. They were greatly rejoiced because they had had such wonderful power, but He seemed to check them, and said, "I will give you something to rejoice for. Rejoice that your names are written in Heaven." He wanted them to know it. Do you think Paul, amid all his difficulties and persecutions, would have gone right on if he hadn't known his name was written in Heaven? Do you think those martyrs would have gone to the stake if they had had any doubt about their salvation? It is the privilege of every child of God to walk in the light—to say, "Abba, Father! Heaven is my home. God is my Father, Jesus Christ is my Saviour." I have just touched some of these great doctrines.

BELIEVE THE BOOK.

In closing, let us take the Book, and let us believe it from beginning to end—every word true—and the words we can't understand, let us believe them.— You that are working in the vineyard, feed on the Word of God. I believe the reason the people won't come more than they do into our churches is because

we don't feed them enough on the Word of God.—
They have been fed on sawdust long enough. For
men who have nothing but essays it is hard to get
pulpits, and it will be harder. The reason there are
so many pulpits vacant is that there isn't men
enough willing to give the Word of God. Go into
one of our city parks in Winter to feed the birds
and throw down a handfull of sawdust. You may
deceive them once, but you won't a second time.—
But throw down crumbs, and they'll sweep them up.
So in the churches, give people the Word of God and
they will know the difference. A man once made
an artificial bee, and thought no one could tell the
difference between that and a real bee. But another
man said he could show the difference. He put the
two bees down on the table, and then put a drop of
honey before them. The real bee went for the
honey There are a great many artificial Christians,
and they don't want the Word of God. They'll go
somewhere else. Well, let them go. For every one
that goes five will take his place. What we want is
to give people the Word of God in season and out of
season. I think we have got to have more expounding. A great many churches have mere exhortations
all the time, and it gets very tiresome. There's got
to be expounding as well as exhortation. I have got
an idea that the Sunday morning services ought to
be given to expounding and the afternoon or Sunday
night given to exhortation or preaching. I believe
that is the reason the Scotch people have got the advantage of us Americans.

THE SCOTCH.

I don't believe there is any place in the world where error has such a slim chance of getting a hold as in Scotland. The Scotch are a most wonderful people. You've got to be careful in preaching to them, or the first thing you know some old woman will come up with her Bible under her shawl, and say: "Here; you said so and so. The Bible says so and so." If you make a misquotation, a Scotchman will straighten you right up; but you might make forty misquotations in an American church and nobody would know the difference. We would have better preaching if people would open their Bibles and see whether a man is preaching the Word of God. In Scotland a minister doesn't think of preaching till everybody has found the text. Go to Dr. Bonar's church, in Glasgow. One of the most impressive scenes is to see 1,200 or 1,300 people, and not a soul but has got a Bible. The old doctor will wait till every one has found the place, then he will tell them what the passage in that place means, and then he goes on to another verse. When I was in London the last time, a solicitor—a lawyer—from Edinburg, came down to London to spend a Sunday there. After I had got through preaching, and had gone back to my little room, he came and said, "I was at Glasgow to hear Dr. Bonar." I said, "I wish you would tell me what he preached about," and he went on and told me. The subject was that passage in Galatians in which Paul tells of his going up to Jerusalem to see Peter. The Doctor, said my friend, just let his imagination loose a little in describing what took place between Paul and Peter. He could imagine that one day Peter said, "Paul, will you take a walk to-day?" "Yes." So, arm-in arm they walk, talking about the Kingdom of God. A little while and they enter the Garden of Gethsemane, and Peter says, "There is the very spot where Christ prayed. John fell asleep there. James right there. I was right there, asleep. I didn't know what He was passing through, though I had never seen Him so sorrowful. When I awoke, an angel stood right there (pointing out the place), and there was Christ, sweating great drops of blood, the blood running down His face—passing through that last agony." The next day Peter turns to Paul and says, "Will you take another walk to-day?" That day they go out towards Calvary, and all at once Peter stops, and says, "There, Paul; this is the very spot where His Cross was. It isn't quite filled up yet. One bleeding thief was hanging there, and the other there. Mary stood right there, John there, and James there. I was on the outskirts of the crowd. I couldn't bear to get near Him that day. I couldn't catch a glimpse of His eye, but just looked on Him. The next day Peter turns to Paul and says: "Paul, shan't we take another walk to-day?" "Yes; I would be very glad." They go out toward Bethany, and suddenly Peter says, "There, Paul; this is the very last spot where I saw Him. We were talking with Him, and all at once I noticed His feet didn't touch the ground, and the last I ever saw of Him, He was up there in the air; and while I stood there, two men—might have been Moses and Elias, I didn't know—appeared and talked to us." Now, don't you think people like that kind of preaching? It will warm up these cold hearts of ours to hear about Christ. Don't you think that literally took place? Nineteen hundred years have passed away, and we go to Jerusalem and try to find these spots; and tell me that while Paul was the guest of Peter he wouldn't take him and show him the very spot where the Lord and Master had gone away to Heaven? I haven't any doubts about it. And what we want is just to take the Scriptures and make them real. That's what we want—to hear about Jesus Christ—and any minister that can feed his people and tell them about Christ is the man I want to hear. That's what we want in our churches. God help you that are preaching to preach the Word of God. Make it as plain as you can. If we had more of the Word of God there would be fewer defalcations and scandals inside the Church. It seems to me the time is coming when there should be a change in the churches of God in this land.

NEW INTEREST—FOREIGN MISSIONS.

NARRATIVE BY MR. J. E. K. STUDD, OF ENGLAND.

The convention closed on Friday night. Most of the delegates started for home next day. The interest waxed greater up to the last moment. Mr. Moody says: "Probably no man has attended more religious meetings than I have in the past ten years, but I never saw anything like this." Day after day fresh arrivals came on every train, and towards the close the accommodations not only of the three buildings of the Young Ladies' Seminary, but those of private residences and farmhouses throughout the neighborhood were taxed to an unprecedented degree. On two or three occasions the large auditorium in Stone Hall was filled to excess. There were fourteen hundred chairs in the room, and yet multitudes were obliged to stand. At first the daily programme was as I described last week; but on the part of many a demand for more meetings arose, till finally there were seven distinct meetings in succession in one day, besides two or three sometimes going on at the same time. The following will afford an idea of the pressure: 7:30, breakfast; 8:00, morning services at Marquand Hall and East Hall; 8:30, meeting in the tent to hear the reports from Christian workers; 10

to 12, service of song and regular meeting at Stone Hall; 12:30, dinner; 1:30, meeting in the tent for prayer and Bible study; 3 to 5, service of song and regular meeting at Stone Hall; 6, supper; 6:30, meeting in the tent; 7:30 to 9, evening services at Marquand Hall and East Hall, or a general meeting at Stone Hall.

The delegates from a distance were, most of them, accommodated with sleeping rooms at Marquand Hall, Stone Hall, and East Hall. Those in the two former took their meals at Marquand Hall. Those in the East Hall, together with transient guests from surrounding towns, took meals in that building. The temporary hotel arrangements of the three buildings were under the supervision of Mr. C. K. Ober, one of the Y. M. C. A. College Secretaries, and most admirably were they managed.

A flutter was caused by the arrival, on Saturday night, of Mr. J. E. K. Studd, of London, England. He was the last captain of the Cambridge eleven of cricketers; and it will remain to his life-long credit, that when Mr. Moody visited Cambridge University, and was in danger of a shower of rotten eggs from the riotous students, he boldly took his seat beside the evangelist on the platform, and accomplished wonders in quelling the disturbance by his personal influence. Mr. Studd is the eldest of three brothers, all famous at cricket; the second of whom, Mr. C. T. Studd, is now in China as one of the leaders of the band of seven missionaries who recently went out in connection with the China Inland Mission. Mr. J. E. K. Studd was entertained by Mr. Moody, and accorded much prominence at the meetings. He was accompanied by his wife, who is a daughter of Lady Beauchamp, and who, like her husband, has a brother (Mr. Montagu Beauchamp) in China.

On Monday night Mr. John B. Gough arrived, and was entertained by Mr. Moody. He gave one of his most eloquent addresses on Wednesday night. Mr. William Noble, the distinguished temperance evangelist of England, who has also been present, spoke the same evening. In fact, almost every country under the sun has been represented. The register shows names from China, India and South Africa.

During the second week Mr. and Mrs. McGranahan arrived, affording a welcome reinforcement to the corps of singers. The male choir of the Boys' School at Mount Hermon acquitted itself remarkably well under the leadership of Mr. Towner. Mr. Sankey, Mr. and Mrs. McGranahan, and Mr. and Mrs. Towner relieved one another at the various services. They were well sustained by a strong volunteer choir; and even the congregation at large seemed to take up the new hymns as if by intuition? The vim and gusto with which these were sung produced an effect that was most inspiring.

Mr. Moody presided at all the regular meetings, and though the strain upon him was tremendous, he looked fresh at the close. In arranging the programme, he seemed to feel his way along, and evidently depended upon the promptings of the Holy Spirit rather than upon any wisdom of his own.

A THRILLING NARRATIVE—ADDRESS BY MR. J. E. K. STUDD.

So much enthusiasm was excited by Mr. Studd's address in East Hall, that it is given here in full. The meeting was for men only, and, at the special request of the ladies, the address was repeated with slight variations at their meeting in Marquand Hall on Tuesday evening. Mr. Studd, on being introduced by Mr. Moody, said:

I want to try to-night to give you a short sketch of the way in which the Lord constrained those seven missionaries, of whom you have doubtless heard, to leave England for China in February last; how the Lord anointed them with power, and what He has been doing through them since He sent them out. First of all, we come to Mr. Moody's and Mr. Sankey's visit to Cambridge in 1883—rather more than two years ago now. There we had large meetings, and certainly some of those men who have gone to China were at that time converted. As I look at their photographs I can pick out those who found Christ for the first time through those meetings. The first man of whom I will speak, Mr. Stanley Smith, was converted about ten years ago. He came down to Cambridge when he heard Mr. Moody was to come there; for he wanted to see and hear the man who had been the means of his conversion some eight years before.

MR. MOODY AT CAMBRIDGE.

At Cambridge, Mr. Moody had a wonderful work, and that work has been going on since; and from those converts a great many of the men who have now offered themselves as missionaries, as well as a great many who are waiting, just waiting their time—from those converts brought to Christ then, these missionary ranks have been filled. One of the men converted at that time—Mr. Swan—was one of the leading men in the Cambridge University eight; and it is a remarkable thing that those seven men who have gone out were all men who have made their mark. I only mention this to let you see the way in which the Lord moves. He doesn't take men haphazard—any sort of men; but He takes men that He means to make something of—men who are just fit to carry on the work as He wants it carried on.

EFFECT OF THE LONDON MEETINGS.

Well, then; Mr. Moody was in London. My brother, who had been in Australia, playing for the English cricket team, and, therefore, hadn't a chance to hear Mr. Moody at Cambridge, when he came to London was constantly at his meetings. And there he was really awakened up. He had been getting rather cold, and though he was a true Christian all the time, hadn't been doing any religious work. But at those meetings what he heard and saw stirred his heart, and immediately he felt that he must set about some kind of work. Mr. Moody set him at work in the inquiry-room, and in the after-meetings. Then he set him at work amongst his own friends, and the Lord at once began to bless him in that line. I shall never forget the joy that filled his heart when the first five men he brought to Mr. Moody's meetings found the Lord Jesus Christ there; and they were five of the leading cricketers we had in England at the time. They were his own friends, and it was an immense encouragement to him. Every moment he could spare from his cricket, or from his work, he used to go to those meetings; and night after night he stayed as long as there were people in the hall to be talked to. Well; his health gave way,—he had hurt himself a little by a certain accident at cricket, and then from hard work—and that summer he could not do much, and he took a rest in the country.

"WHAT WILT THOU HAVE ME TO DO?"

One thing troubled him. He was training for the bar—had passed his examination at Cambridge, and the trial examination for the English bar, and was intending to practice law. But he felt that he had enough to live upon, and didn't want to occupy his life in making money; he just wanted to be given up to the Lord. Yet he could not make out what the Lord wanted him to do. I think the pressure upon his mind in trying to find out what he ought to do rather kept him back from getting his full health. However, he stayed out in the country for some time resting. After a while he came back again to London, well; but the same difficulty troubled him. He consulted among his friends about it, and their advice was, as far as human advice could go, that he should wait till the Lord should clearly point the way, and, in the meantime, go on at the work he was doing, so as not to lose any time, whatever happened. But he could not turn his thoughts to anything else. At last he made up his mind he would just take the words in the first chapter of Acts—the commission Christ gave to His disciples: "But ye shall receive power, after that the Holy Ghost is come upon you; and ye shall be witnesses unto Me, both into Jerusalem, and in all Judea, and in Samaria, and unto the uttermost part of the earth." Then he just practically shut himself up from every one, and spent day after day in his own room, seeking an enduement of power from on High, and seeking guidance. I don't know how long—I think it was two days or more—that he kept himself in his room (except two hours a day which he spent in exercise), reading the Bible, and the Bible alone—spent the whole time in reading that Bible and in praying, asking God what he would have him to do.

DECIDING TO GO TO CHINA.

In one way and another China was brought before him. He had reached a state of mind that he was willing to stay in England or go to China, or go anywhere, so long as he got his orders from the Lord. I don't know how he came to think of China. No one spoke to him; no one even knew what he was doing—I didn't know myself till afterwards. But somehow or other the idea that he must go to China was thrust upon him, and he could not get out of it. Then he heard that Mr. Stanley Smith had decided to go to China; he had seen his way perfectly clear about six months before, perhaps longer. Mr.

Stanley Smith came one day and told my brother that he was going to the China Inland Mission prayer meeting at Mildmay Park. Mr. Martin was going to be there, and a man was going to speak who had walked across China by himself, and my brother thought he must be something of a man who could do that. He went to hear him, and all the time seemed to be getting his mind more and more on China. The word kept ringing in his ears. He went, I say, to the meeting, and heard this man speak; and there the claims of China came home to him, and God just seemed to call him right there and then. He came home late at night; and I well remember how startled I was when he told me for the first time that he was going to China. I don't know that I ever had such a blow. You can imagine that it was an awful wrench, coming upon me, as it did, so suddenly. I said I thought we had better make it a matter of prayer. I didn't believe it was quite clear. I thought he had been wrought up to an excitement at that meeting, and that the impression might pass away. So we just knelt in prayer together and asked the Lord to make it perfectly clear what my brother should do, and if it was His will that he should go to China, to remove every single doubt from our minds. Then my brother went to bed. Ordinarily he got to sleep directly his head touched the pillow—for usually he was working hard at one thing or another—but that night he could not really sleep, but rather dozed. He would wake up every two hours, and when he slept it was only a sort of dozing. And every time he woke up, that verse, which he hadn't read for some time, certainly not for months, that verse in the second Psalm: "Ask of Me, and I shall give thee the heathen for thine inheritance, and the uttermost parts of the earth for thy possession," kept ringing through his mind. In the morning he said it was perfectly clear to him what the Lord had for him to do—that he had got to go to China. Of course, I couldn't say any more; I could not say, "Don't go." That was the first thing that started him off.

MISSIONARY MEETINGS IN CAMBRIDGE.

Well, then; after that they went up to Cambridge—my brother, Mr. Stanley Smith, Mr. Hudson Taylor, and several others. First of all, Mr. Stanley Smith went up and held some preliminary meetings, and stirred up a considerable interest among the students, he and my brother working amongst them; and then they had a meeting not only for the students, but for townspeople, at which they spoke, and others as well. Mr. Hudson Taylor presented the claims of China, and the work of the China Inland Mission. The result of that work was that over thirty men—certainly thirty men if not more—offered themselves definitely for Christian work, and not only Christian work in England, but wherever the Lord would have them to go. Some of them have gone. One of them now is out in South Africa, and is working his way inland there; others are in China. One man, Mr. Polhill-Turner, gave himself up; and his brother, who was in the Grenadier Guards at the time, determined to do so as soon as he could. For the time there was an obstacle; he had only joined the regiment three weeks before, and he was afraid he could not resign his commission; but that matter was arranged.

MEETINGS AT OXFORD.

Well, after that, Mr. Stanley Smith and my brother went to Oxford, and there they met with great success. A wonderful interest was stirred up. Quite a number—I cannot say how many—decided there and then to give themselves also for foreign mission work, ready to do whatever the Lord would have for them to do. Amongst the students there was a prominent leader in athletics—McLean by name—a rower in the Oxford eight, and a leading man in that crew. In Oxford, perhaps, we hadn't been so fortunate in getting hold of the leading men of the University, as we had been at Cambridge. You know, at college, in order for a man to be much thought of, he must be good at athletics or something else. Let me explain. In England, for a man to be good at athletics is a great honor. In this country it is just the other way. Well, continued the speaker, what I mean is, that a man must either be good at athletics or good in something. Here was this fellow, anyhow. He was one of the first men in the University in the line of boating. He was in the audience at one of the meetings held by Mr. Stanley Smith and my brother. The Lord touched his heart there in some way or another. He was not just then brought into the clear knowledge of salvation; but the Word so reached his heart that he wrote a check and sent it to the China Inland Mission, to the amount of £10. The secretary was rather struck with his letter—he was lead from something this man said to imagine somehow that he hadn't got peace. So, in sending an acknowledgment, he wrote a long letter to him putting the way of peace before him; and the result of that letter was that he accepted Christ and came into full peace. It so happened that at that time Mr. McLean had to go right down to Mortlake, where the whole crew were known, and where the race was to take place in a few days. After the race was finished Mr. McLean held a mission service at Mortlake. The race was on Saturday, and he held this meeting on Sunday. One of the best rowers in the Cambridge eight—the Mr. Swan of whom I have already spoken—heard that this meeting was to be held, and he went up to attend it, taking others with him. Mr. Swan is a man who is wonderfully good at anything he takes up, and he is going as a missionary himself—I think it will be to Africa or China. Well; as a result of that meeting, two of the Cambridge crew united for the Lord Jesus Christ. The brother of one of them has since followed his example; and he was a member of the Dragoon Guards—in a position which would be recognized amongst young fellows in the country.

MR. STUDD AND MR. STANLEY SMITH IN SCOTLAND.

Well, then; after those meetings, my brother and Mr. Stanley Smith started for Scotland. They started off in rather an extreme fashion—at least it seemed so to us, and yet it seemed to one also that it was the Lord's leading; He brought them around to a different way of thinking afterwards, but he led them then. They gave up everything—never considered their means of living; but just went off carrying what they had—one coat or suit of clothes —and went to Scotland in that way. It just shows that if we are willing to leave all for His sake, God will bless us. Well; they went off in this way, and God just worked most marvelously with them. You have heard somewhat of the work in Scotland. At Edinburg they held meetings first for two nights, and then they took a large place, and held a meeting at which there must have been two thousand undergraduates present. There never had been such an assembly of University students in Endinburg, and

SUCH INTEREST WAS NEVER KNOWN.

When my brother and Mr. Stanley Smith spoke, the Lord seemed to be working with them—the Lord touched those men's hearts. The interest only deepened after they had gone. Then they went to Glasgow. Great interest was created in every audidience in the same way. Wherever they went the Lord was with them, and there were the most wonderful conversions. Let me give you a striking case. A young fellow read that my brother was to be present at a meeting in one of the places in the north of England he went to. This young fellow was accustomed to go to places of a very different sort; but he thought he would go to this meeting. A friend chaffed him a little about it, saying, "I hear you are going to help Mr. Studd pray to-night." They laughed together and thought it was a good joke. But he went to the meeting, and the Lord met him there, and he was converted. I could tell you more of the most striking cases of the Lord working through them. They were not speakers— well, Mr. Stanley Smith was a speaker, but my brother was not—not an orator anyway. But the Lord seemed to be with them in those audiences in a wonderful degree.

A SECOND VISIT TO EDINBURG.

Just before they left England they thought they would go up to those Edinburg fellows again; and they were there for, I think, five nights, and the interest was deeper than ever. It had gone on growing. Those who had decided for the Lord had continued steadfast, and had been witnesses for Him. And now the movement culminated, and as a result of those five nights' work, one hundred and twenty of those Edinburg students have given up their long vacation, and are preaching the Gospel in different cities, towns, and villages in England and Scotland. They have been sending from time to time three or four members as embassies from one University to another in term time. Some go to Edinburg from Glasgow, and then some from Glasgow to Edinburg, and so on in the different Universities—stirring one another up, and telling of the things the Lord has done for them.

A WONDERFUL MEETING IN LONDON.

Well; then they came back to London, and first we held a meeting in Eccleston Hall. Then it was arranged to hold a meeting in Exeter Hall. A good many did not believe the hall would be filled. It was only taken practically a week before the time. The Young Men's Christian Association were to have conducted the meeting; but they thought the hall could not be filled, and then, perhaps, they had a good many other things to attend to, so that the China Inland Mission found they must take it and work the whole thing. The hall holds about 3,000, and people thought it would be rather a good thing if it should be anywhere near filled. Instead of that, half an hour before the time there wasn't a seat to be had. The whole of the seven men who were going out to China spoke, and the effect was very marked. I saw one of the secretaries of the Young Men's Christian Association the other day, and he says, day by day, they are hearing of the results of that meeting. Every day they hear something about it. And then the next day, and every day since that, the China Inland Mission have had their tables packed with letters—so many that they could not answer them—from men applying to go to China. You see how the Lord worked with them.

THE VOYAGE TO CHINA.

And now I will just tell you a little about the voyage out—how wonderfully the Lord blessed them there. They went across the Continent and joined their ship, the Kaisar-i-Hund, at Suez. On the ship there was a man who was noted as an awful character. He was captain of a merchantman. He had come home, leaving his vessel at Calcutta, and in a fortnight had quarreled with every one of his friends, put on his hat and taken his passage without even saying farewell to any one of them; and now he was going out on this same ship. He was exactly the same up to Suez, and was known all through the ship as a drunken, swearing, infidel man—so much so that a Christian soldier in the same cabin with him was nearly driven mad with his terrible swearing and bad language. One of the stewards was heard to say that he didn't believe at all in religion, but if that man was converted, he would begin to think something about it. This swearing captain was so pleased when he heard that the missionaries were coming on board that he rubbed his hands with glee, because he thought he would turn them into such ridicule—he was so delighted with the thought of the fun he would have. The first day the missionaries came on board some of them

WENT UP TO THIS MAN

without knowing much about him, and asked him if he ever read the Bible. He snapped them right off, and said it was all rubbish. Then Mr. Hoste asked him if he would read the Bible with him. "Oh, yes," he said; and so they would read the Bible together—the missionary talking and trying to meet the infidel's objections. But he didn't seem to produce any effect. After two days my brother was led to go and speak to this man. For an hour, perhaps two hours, he talked with him; and he says that he never met with such a mass of infidel objections and arguments. No way was made, and it seemed as if the whole thing was utterly hopeless. However, my brother felt he couldn't give up talking to this man. Breathing a prayer for Divine guidance, he turned to him again, and said: "Well; I know that I have got a peace that passeth all understanding, and a joy that is unspeakable. I can't explain to you how great it is." The man was startled. "Have you?" said he; "you are an awfully lucky fellow. Hundreds have been seeking that all their lives, and haven't found it." And then my brother told him that the secret of his peace and joy was a simple trust in Jesus, and nothing else; and told him how he could get it. The man began to pour out his heart to him. He found the missionary had something he wanted, and he opened up his heart to him at once—so much so that my brother asked him then and there to decide for Christ. He could not decide then, he said. "Go down to your cabin, then," said my brother. He went down to his cabin, and there and then on his knees

HE DID ACCEPT THE LORD JESUS CHRIST.

And the first thing he did was to write home to his friends and ask forgiveness for leaving them as he had done. Then he publicly bore witness to the ship's company. And he *was* a witness—he was a changed man. He bore testimony out-and-out by a changed life, and it stirred the whole ship—from the captain down to the very lowest on the vessel, either as passenger or as servant—just to hear this man, and to see the change that the Lord had wrought in him. And the last I heard of him was, that he had been restored to his position in India as captain of a merchant ship, and he was witnessing there for the Lord Jesus Christ just the same. So you see God thus added His seal to the work of these men. And this was not the only man who was saved on that ship. There were thirteen second-class passengers in all; and every one of these thirteen professed to have become Christians before they left the ship.

At Colombo the missionaries had to change to another ship. They joined the Verona, and on that voyage the presence of the Lord was again manifest. There were conversions amongst the men, and one of the last things that happened on board the ship was this: There was a steward who was sick. My brother had a talk with him, and he was stirred. That man found Christ; and before they left the ship the Lord had converted also another steward.

REMARKABLE MEETINGS IN SHANGHAI.

They came to Shanghai, and my brother caused to be given to every one of the stewards and passengers a copy of Miss Havergal's book, "The Royal Invitation." You would think that after a month's voyage the people of the ship would have become pretty tired of the missionaries, for they had all been at them, one after the other. Not so. Every one of the whole ship's company went to the meetings in Shanghai. And they were the most wonderful meetings that were ever known in the history of the city. A little while before that Mr. Douglass had held some meetings; but they dwindled till they had to be given up. The meetings started by the missionaries were held every night, and they were held not only in one place, but in several halls in different parts of the town at the same time. They were held every night for about three weeks; and night after night the interest increased, and the numbers increased. On the first Monday night, after my brother had been speaking to the people about salvation, he said he thought that if any one had received such a wonderful gift from the Lord Jesus Christ, the least he could do would be to confess it; and he asked any one there—every one there—who had accepted Christ and found in Him a joy and peace that they had never found in anything else, to rise and say so. He had no sooner done speaking than

UP JUMPED A CLERGYMAN

and said he had been a great sinner, and of course this startled everybody, for he was the Church of England clergyman of the place, and the incumbent of the cathedral there, and had been respected by everybody. My brother says he never heard such a testimony in his life. He told them just shortly and simply how he had tried all his life to do his duty, how he had taken great interest in his work and tried to do everything in the best way; yet, he said, if the Lord had called for his soul on Sunday night he would have been a lost man. Now he thanked God he was saved. He had never spent such a Sunday night, lying awake in agony under his deep conviction of sin. But he had found peace by just trusting in Christ as his Lord and his Saviour. The following day there appeared in the Shanghai *Courier*—perhaps the leading paper there—a very bitter article cutting up this clergyman—cutting up his testimony, and saying it was quite impossible that he should continue in the cathedral. Referring to my brother, it said something to this effect: "Mr. Studd has asked the question 'Why should he not have left England?' As Mr. Studd has asked this question we will try to answer it for him. He had no right to leave England. He should have considered his influence there," and all that. The morality of the Chinese, said the editor, was quite as good as that of Christian nations. It was a most bitter article, and other parts of the paper showed the same spirit. Says my brother: "We could not understand it at first; but we found a reason for it afterwards. It turned out that the editor's wife had been to the meetings, and was converted. She told her husband, and he was so angry that he sat up and wrote those articles for the Shanghai *Courier*. Well, a day or two afterwards the editor himself was induced to attend the meetings, and

HE, TOO, FOUND THE LORD JESUS CHRIST.

Then these missionaries went around to the different stations, and they had a conference at Gan-K'ing, up the Yang-tse river. They had wonderful blessings, and the Lord seemed just pouring out His Spirit upon all the missionaries, stirring them up. Then they separated, and Mr. Stanley Smith went up to Pekin, while my brother went up the Yang-tse, and is now going on up that river. Mr. Stanley Smith is doing some remarkable work in gathering and uniting the missionaries of the different missionary societies together. He started first in Tientsin to hold a meeting for daily prayer; and the missionaries of all the different sects took part in it— nearly all. The only one that kept out of it was the Society for the Propagation of Christian Knowledge. In Pekin he came across one of the London missionaries—a physician who was very able, and had the *entree* into the palace of the leading man— practically the King—of Chi-Li, on account of his knowledge and skill. Mr. Stanley Smith and this medical man got talking about faith-healing. The medical man was not clear about it, yet he was interested in the subject. He thought man ought to use the means God had put at his disposal; but wherever man could not do anything, there faith-healing was a legitimate recourse. And as he was taking Mr. Stanley Smith with him on his rounds, he came up to a man suffering from epileptic fits. Said he: "Now, there is a proper case for faith-healing. I can do nothing for that man." Mr. Stanley Smith said: "Let us get down and pray about him." They knelt down there, putting their hands upon him and praying—just believing in the Lord for this man. And the next day that man was at the meetings. In a week

HE WAS PERFECTLY WHOLE,

and he has been whole ever since. This was one of the results of the work there.

Well, then; I have had some very interesting letters from my brother. His party is going up the river Han. The Chinese sometimes call the missionaries "Jesus Christ disciples," but more generally "foreign devils." The people are intensely curious to see them. They can't show their faces at all. If they go out they are followed by about two hundred people all around them. If a ship anchors, people put their sticks in the port-hole, and if the missionaries put up curtains to hide themselves they won't take that for an answer, but dig with their sticks till they have got a hole, and get a good stare. My brother was very much struck with the fact that these men are all religious. Before they leave port with a ship they offer sacrifice, and never start without sacrificing a rooster. It is very extraordinary to find the old ceremonies in the Bible out there. As one letter after another comes to me from my brother, each is more full of joy than the other. His only regret is that he hadn't gone out sooner.

OUR DUTY AT HOME.

Now, what can we do? Well, I will tell you what we are doing in England. We don't forget to pray for the missionaries. They are always wanting prayer. Missionaries are exposed to temptations such as our life is not. It is not all easy after they have cut themselves off from the world, as we are apt to suppose. The world follows them in their hearts, and they want prayer for power to conquer the superstitions with which they come in contact. Some of us have started a meeting in London every

Wednesday. We meet together on Wednesday at five o'clock for one hour, and engage in prayer for those men. Then there is another thing. Mr. Moody showed you yesterday a text (referring to a beautiful piece of needlework) which was done by a lady who was a cripple. She wanted very much to do something for the work, and her part was this. Many of your ladies here can work these texts, and they will do a great deal of good. And then again, a gentleman has written and persuaded a hundred people to remember those missionaries in prayer every Saturday, and so these hundred people pray, and we have this meeting on Monday as well. And so I think that here in America some of you could start a meeting, just praying for these missionaries and other missionaries all over the world, and asking the Lord for the power of the Holy Spirit upon them. Some of us will probably find in our prayers we are sent out ourselves. Well, we shall thank God if we are. But anyway, let us join our prayers to the prayers of those who are already beseeching God in behalf of those missionaries, asking Him for fresh power, that He may keep them and bless them.

REMARKS BY MR. MOODY.

Mr. Moody exhibited a photograph of the seven missionaries in Chinese costume, saying: "These men have taken the costume of the country while they are there. They are picked men every one of them. They are leaders of society, and held positions very high. It seems to me we are getting back to apostolic times. Now let us bow our heads and pray for these seven missionaries. Let there be just one cry going up to God for these seven men." Dr. Pierson led in prayer.

Mr. Moody said: "I suppose, friends, you see where this dear brother got his power. It was in those ten days alone with God; and how that ought to encourage us to get along with God and get power. I don't believe it is the mind of God we should be toiling all night and catching nothing. I don't believe it is the mind of God we should be praying and working without results. I believe what God did for that young man He will do for us. Speaking of the work at Cambridge, I don't think the preaching had anything to do with it. We received a pressing invitation—Mr. Sankey and I—to go to Cambridge when we were in England ten years ago, and I refused. I thought I had got no call to go to universities. But when we were over there again, another call came, signed by a list of names six or eight feet long; and I said: 'I will go.' The first Sunday night we were in Cambridge the students tried to break the meeting up. I had preached to all classes of people—to the hoodlums of California—and never had that happen before. It looked very much as if they were going to snatch the whole thing out of our hands. I don't believe there were fifty students out of that roomful that heard the songs of Mr. Sankey, and right on through the whole meeting it was just the same. On Monday night the disturbance was just as bad, or worse. On Tuesday the outlook was darker than ever. But on that day a lady—a bedridden saint—who was very much interested in the work, sent around an invitation to a few Christians to get together in a little upper room and plead with God for a change in those students. That turned the tide. It wasn't the preaching. They had heard better sermons. They had had sermons from the best preachers of the Church of England. It was those Christians in that upper room praying with God that made the difference. And how they did pray! It seemed as if their prayers burst into Heaven, and I said, 'The victory is ours.' That night I preached. I don't think I had much power. When I ask, 'If any man in this audience wants to become a Christian, will you go into the inquiry room?'—they had their gowns on—of course they were known—if you know anything about universities you know it is pretty hard to get them moved. When I gave this invitation I didn't know there would be a man. But there was a hush over that audience, and

FIFTY-TWO MEN SPRANG TO THEIR FEET,

and went up in that gallery, and that night we had all the inquirers we could attend to. About one o'clock—I was getting pretty tired—a man came to me, saying, 'I wish you would come and talk to this man.' They were on their faces, crying to God for mercy. God had broken not only their stubborn wills, but their hearts were broken. It wasn't the preaching; the preaching was pretty weak that night. I talked to this man, and the tears were running down his cheeks; but he found Christ that night. Some one said to me, 'Do you know who that was? That is the head wrangler in Cambridge,' the highest in books. Among the three thousand students at Cambridge he was the best—the leader. There he was on his knees, and the power of God just came in answer to prayer. Next Sunday night there were two hundred or three hundred broken hearts, of men who wanted to be for God.

"It isn't preaching we want; it is prayer. I would rather be able to pray like David than to preach with the eloquence of Gabriel. We don't want any more preachers in this country—we have got enough. What we want is to pray. Let us open up communication with Heaven, and the blessing will come down."

THE BOOK OF BOOKS?

At the close of Mr. Moody's address on Thursday forenoon, Dr. Pierson, of Philadelphia, at his request, followed for ten minutes. Isaiah, said he, is divided in the original, into three portions, each ending with a mournful refrain concerning the wicked. These refrains will be found at the end of the forty-eighth chapter; of the fifty-seventh, and of the whole book. When God divided the book into three portions he must have meant something; and so in the center of the middle portion we find that wonderful piece of poetry, the crown-jewel, the blood-red ruby, the fifty-third chapter. In the British Navy there is a scarlet thread running through every line of cordage, and though a rope be cut into inch pieces, it can be recognized as belonging to the Government. So is there a scarlet thread running all through the Bible; the whole book points to Christ. In the promise made to Adam, appears, as it were, the first twig of a tree. Twig after twig is added, till we can count not only two hundred direct promises of the Messiah, but fifteen hundred direct and indirect. Then, as history comes to fulfill these predictions, each little twig in turn is set on fire, yet not consumed, till finally the whole tree becomes a great burning bush, and we take off our shoes and stand in awe, for it is holy ground. The speaker was born in a Christian family, father and mother Christians, a brother a minister, a sister married to a minister. He was educated for the ministry, and entered it not fully conscious of his responsibility. His first pastorate was among a very hornet's nest of infidels. They talked with him and lent him books. Having imbibed his belief merely from his Christian surroundings, as a matter of tradition, he was unable to meet this onset. His faith in the inspiration of the Bible, in the Divinity of Christ, and in his own salvation, was shaken, till he became alarmed. Then he went over the whole ground, getting down to the very foundation, and it was not long till he not only believed more firmly than ever, but knew why.

In the afternoon the subject was the Bible, and how to use it. Mr. L. D. Wishard, General College Young Men's Christian Association Secretary, spoke first for a few minutes. If the Bible, he said, is the sword of the Spirit, we ought to use it as a sword. When an infidel makes light of the Word of God, stick it right into him. If he doesn't mind it much, keep on—stick it in harder and harder. As the Duke of Wellington said, the side will win that can keep on hammering longest.

HOW TO STUDY THE BIBLE.

The Rev. Wm. Walton Clark, of Staten Island, then offered a few "Helpful Suggestions in Bible Study." The following were his points, each of which was amplified with copious citations from

Scripture: 1. Study, believing that God will reward us. In proportion as we diligently seek God through His Word, will He reward our efforts. 2. Study, believing the Holy Ghost is our Teacher. He who wrote the Word is most competent to teach it. It is one thing to be familiar with the geography, chronology, and history of the Bible; it is another to understand its underlying spiritual principles? Man can teach much that is on the surface, but only the Holy Ghost can teach the deep hidden things of God. 3. Study to find Christ in all the Scriptures. Each book in the Bible has Christ for its centre and object. The disciples thought they knew the Scriptures? but they did not see Jesus in them, for the Lord rebuked them for their failure in this very particular. 4. Study, believing that all Scripture is fully and equally inspired. The great theological question of the day is whether the Bible is wholly inspired, partly inspired, or not inspired at all. Even among theologians there is a great difference of opinion; and as these opinions are ventilated in the secular and religious press, it is our duty to look into the question deeply, that we may not only be convinced ourselves, but be able to convince others also. We believe in the full verbal inspiration of Holy Writ; that the Scriptures as they originally came from the hands of the writers were in truth "God-breathed" (2 Tim. iii, 16, 17). Bishop Ryle says: "Give me the plenary verbal theory with all its difficulties, rather than the doubt. I accept the difficulties, and humbly wait for their solution; but while I wait I am standing on a rock." Let a man become weak on inspiration, and he will surely slide further and further from the truth. 5. Study, believing that all Scripture was written for *us*; designed for our personal benefit and growth in grace. Paul says, in Rom. xv, 4, that these things were written for *our* learning, that *we* might have hope. Again, in 1 Cor. x, 11, he says, after giving an outline of events in the history of Israel: "All these things happened unto them for ensamples, and they are written for *our* admonition." This history, then, has a present value for our souls. 6. Study, to learn the scope of truth, its range and design. As we take up each portion, let us inquire, What was the design of God in writing this particular book? For what special purpose was this Gospel, Epistle, or prophecy written? And we often find the key to the book in the first verse, as in Isaiah, Matthew, John, and Revelation. Ascertain the design. Genesis is a book of beginnings; Exodus, of redemptions; Leviticus, of sacrifice and priesthood; Numbers, of walk in the wilderness; Deuteronomy, of conduct for Canaan; Joshua, of warfare. Miles Coverdale says, in the preface of his Bible of 1535: "It will greatly help you to understand Scripture if you mark not only what is written, but of whom, and to whom; with what words, at what time, where, of what intent, with what circumstances, considering that which goes before and that which follows." 7. Rightly divide the Word of Truth. There is an old Latin proverb: "Distinguish the periods, and the Scriptures will harmonize." We must see the difference between the dispensations of law and of grace; between the earthly blessings in the Old Testament and the spiritual blessings in the New. Let the student locate in each dispensation—past, present and future—such portions of Scripture as belong to it; then will the revealed Word harmonize, and the word of prophecy become more sure.

The Rev. S. H. Pratt, evangelist, recommended marking one's Bible with marginal notes, so as to make the great truths stand out prominently. Illuminated minds displayed the choicest texts in bright colors, and on this principle should we render salient the passages of special importance. The Rev. C. M. Southgate, of Worcester, strongly recommended studying the Bible, book by book. Dr. Pierson referred to the one hundred and nineteenth Psalm, pointing out that it is a sacred acrostic, divided into sections according to the letters of the Hebrew alphabet, each section containing eight verses, and each of those verses beginning in the Hebrew with the letter of that section. This he took to indicate that all literature cannot express the Word of God. See the numerous synonyms in this Psalm for "word." Get at the specific aim of each book. The key to Hebrews is "better" (xi, 40). The key to Ecclesiastes is, that man is too big for the world. From the earthly point of view alone, his life is a failure. There must be the spiritual half-hinge, or hemisphere, to join with the earthly half-hinge, or hemisphere, that will round out the whole.

THE RISEN CHRIST.

On Friday, the Rev. Dr. Gordon, of Boston, spoke in the forenoon on "The Risen Life of Christ." The

Bible, he said, sets forth with much fullness the present life of Christ—Hebrews and Revelation being especially rich concerning it. The first phase of the present life of Christ is the fact that He is seated. That is His attitude because His work is finished. The only place where the risen Lord is not represented as seated is at the stoning of Stephen. Stephen sees Him standing, and it would seem as if He had risen from His seat to behold the first martyrdom. At such a sight He could not sit still. Always, elsewhere, however, He is seated. This is of interest to us, because it would appear to render Him more accessible. If you go to a man at his office, in business hours, you will find him very busy; hardly able to spare you a minute. But take him when his work is finished, at home, seated by his fireside, and how much more likely are you to gain his ear! The Jews observed the Passover with sandals on their feet, loins girded, and staff in hand; but the Lord's Supper of the present dispensation is partaked of seated, because of Christ's finished work. This shows the significance of even little things in the ceremonies and forms of the Old and New Testaments. The second phase of the risen life of Christ is His attitude of expectation—expecting the Kingdom. He is seated at the right hand of God till the Kingdom shall be delivered to Him. As in other places, we have fellowship with Him in that. The third phase is His attitude of rest. "There remaineth a rest for the people of God." There are two rests: the rest of grace and the rest of glory. The rest of grace is that which belongs to the believer, because the grace of God is doing for him in Christ what he could not do for himself. But the rest of glory is the rest that comes to the toil-worn child of God, who has been working with all his might, not that he may be saved, but because he *is* saved. We are to be rewarded for our works. A man cannot be rewarded for what he never performed. Christ wrought our salvation. The reward hence refers exclusively to the labor of the dutiful child of God seeking to do the will of Christ. Another phase is, that Christ is confessing us before the Father. Let it be clearly understood that we can and do make it hard for Christ to confess us. For as the devil of old came into the presence of God accusing Job, so now the devil in a sense enters the courts of Heaven accusing us before the Father. Here is some poor, trembling, faltering sinner, who walks unworthy of the vocation whereunto he is called. The devil comes before God, and says: "Ah, yes; that is one of Yours—who promised to serve You and be faithful, and yet see how he is living." Christ's reply is, "Well, he has confessed Me before men, and I promised to confess him before My Father. Yes; he is one of Mine, and I am hoping that this and that will remove every trace of evil." It is a hard thing for Christ to confess us in the face of our many inconsistencies, but He is faithful to His promise. The last phase is Christ interceding for us. "If any man sin we have an advocate," etc. "He ever liveth," etc.

The Rev. W. W. Clark spoke briefly on the relation between cross and crown. Only by bearing our cross can we hope to be with Christ in glory. Mr. Moody said: "That reminds me of a story. A young man once gave a discourse, in the presence of a good old bishop, telling how he had been in Palestine, and stopped at Jerusalem, Bethlehem, Bethany, and ever so many places where Christ was. There was a silence of a moment, when the old bishop rose and said, 'I'd rather be five minutes with Christ than a year in places where He once was.'"

Dr. Pentecost dwelt a moment on the fact that we are members of the body of Christ. He took our nature, and we share His triumph over the grave.

HARMONY OF THE BIBLE.

In the afternoon the Rev. Mr. Clark gave an address on the development of doctrine concerning Christ in the Gospels. In Matthew we see Him as the Messiah; in Mark, as a servant; in Luke, as the Son of Man; in John, as the Son of God. Messiahship, service, humanity, Christianity. Thus we can go through the whole New Testament.

Dr. Gordon then spoke. Man, he said, is forgiven in the New Testament on different ground from that in the Old. In the Old Testament it was because He is merciful. He had made a covenant of mercy. Hence the prophet could appeal to Him not to disgrace the throne of His glory (see Jer. xiv, 20, 21); "We acknowledge, O Lord, our wickedness, and the iniquity of our fathers; for we have sinned against Thee. Do not abhor us, for Thy name's sake; do not disgrace the throne of Thy glory;

remember, break not the throne of Thy covenant with us." But in the New Testament the forgiveness of sins is based on God's justice. Christ has paid the penalty and satisfied the law, and now God forgives sin because He is just. "He is faithful and *just* to forgive us our sins." If He should fail to forgive a man in the present dispensation who asks for pardon in Christ's name, He would disgrace His throne. Another difference between the Old and the New Testaments, is that under the old dispensation a man was righteous at the *end* of works and sacrifices; under the new, Christ having done all, he is righteous at the *beginning*, and thence proceeds to work on. It is now possible to be righteous at the beginning of one's life rather than at the end of it. Again, in the Old Testament man repented and then was forgiven. Now he is forgiven already, and the repentance comes afterwards. A man once was convicted and sentenced to death. A friend interceded, and procured a pardon from the Governor. Taking it to the prison, before showing it, he asked the condemned man what he would do if he got free. In a rage he said he would shoot the judge who sentenced him, and the false witnesses who testified against him. Sorrowfully turning away, the friend went out with the pardon still in his pocket, and tore it up. The man was pardoned, but he would not repent, and the pardon could not be applied. Christ expiated the sins of the world on the Cross, and God was reconciled to us. Now the message is: "Be ye reconciled to God." The idea that we have to go through a long course of repentance keeps back too many. All we have to do is to accept the salvation already purchased and now offered.

Dr. Pierson said the unity of the Bible was that of an organic body: the smallest part could not be destroyed without destroying the symmetry of the whole. The Bible is one grand orchestral chorus, in which the various singers pursue a succession of parts, closing in one great burst of melody from Heaven and earth combined in the apocalypse.

Dr. Pentecost emphasized the amazing love of God to us in that, without waiting for our repentance, He prepared the conditions for our pardon, and then sent the good news of salvation. How did we receive that message? We even killed Him who brought it. Even in the Old Testament may be seen this abounding love: "Because the Lord loved you." (Deut. vii, 7, 8.) He accomplished redemption. The work of Christ is finished and perfect. Why not accept it?

At the evening meeting in East Hall, Dr. Pierson said: What is the matter with our churches? The trouble is, in too many of them, the truth from Heaven is obscured by windows of man's device, and turned into "dim, religious light." These windows are carved, and stained, and decorated till the light cannot get through. We ought to be uncolored panes of glass, through which the light can freely pass. When he was a pastor in Detroit, on a lovely November evening, in one of the leading churches in the city, distinguished for wealth and culture, there were only twenty-five persons around the preacher. The same state of affairs prevailed in

Philadelphia to an alarming extent. Bethany Church, however, had always been filled since it was founded. The remedy for empty churches, he believed, is to give the people God's Word.

PRIVILEGES OF BELIEVERS—GOSPEL TENTS—MR. MOODY ON SINGING—A CLUSTER OF SERMONS.

"THE THREE-FOLD SONSHIP."

On Saturday forenoon, the Rev. Dr. Gordon, of Boston, spoke on "The Three-Fold Sonship." The miracle of all miracles, he said, is our becoming the sons of God. One way to realize our relation as such is to follow the life of Jesus Christ Himself. Whatever is true of Christ is true of every believer—of the body of Christ. Then open the Scriptures. John says Christ was the only-begotten Son of God. This was true when John so wrote; it isn't true now. Afterwards Christ is spoken of as the *first*-begotten—the first-begotten among many brethren. God has appointed Him heir of all things, but He won't have the inheritance alone; we are heirs with Him. Is it not remarkable that the Gospel of John opens with Jesus Christ in the bosom of the Father, and closes with John in the bosom of the Master—the sinner in the bosom of the Saviour?

BEGOTTEN OF GOD.

First: Christ, as the Son of God, was begotten of the Holy Ghost. Said the Angel to Mary: "The power of the Holy Ghost shall come upon thee . . . . therefore that holy thing which shall be born of thee shall be called the Son of God." Yet, notwithstanding it was announced He was to be the Son of God, during all the days of His youth and early manhood there wasn't a single person who knew Him as the Son of God. Who would be most likely to know? John the Baptist, son of prayer, did you know He was the Son of God? "I knew Him not; but when I saw the Holy Spirit resting upon Him, then I knew." John the Evangelist, you have written a great deal about Him, what did you know? "He was in the world .... and the world knew Him not." Did His mother know? Finding Him in the Temple, she said, "Son"—she knew He was *her* son; but when He said, "Wist ye not that I must be about my Father's business?" she understood not the saying which He spake. Up to the time of His public baptism Jesus Christ was in the world as the Son of God, and the world knew Him not. In this we are like Him. 1 John iii, 1: "Behold, what manner of love the Father hath bestowed upon us, that we should be called the sons of God: therefore the world knoweth us not, because it knew Him not." Leavitt said: "The world knoweth us not because we are children of a king. They don't understand the court language." We are sons of God because, like Christ, begotten of the Holy Ghost. "Except a man be born again," etc. Heaven is our home. There is a beautiful kind of water-insect whose natural home is on the earth, but which goes down and feeds at the bottom of the lakes. It carries with it a certain amount of atmospheric air, enough to last an hour or two; and so while it is down there in the mud it is all the time breathing the upper air. Jesus came down here, but all the while He breathed the air of Heaven. So it is with us. Lady Powerscourt said: "The Christian is not looking up from earth to Heaven; he is looking down from Heaven to earth." That little insect was surrounded by marine animals, living and breathing from the water, but the insect breathed a very different air. Our citizenship, our home, our life, is in Heaven. "*Now* are we the sons of God." So far as salvation is concerned, the Scripture knows nothing of future texts. "Ye are no more strangers and foreigners, but fellow-citizens." You are just as truly sons of God the moment you believe on Christ, as you ever will be. No matter whether the world knows it or not. Many years ago, one of the kings of England was in exile. One night sleeping in a hay-mow, another night cooking his own supper; yet all the time son of a king, having the right to sit on the throne. Nobody knew him, but he was just as truly the son of a king.

DIVINELY CERTIFIED.

Secondly: Christ was witnessed. "The Holy Ghost descended in a bodily shape like a dove upon Him; and a voice came from Heaven, which said, "Thou art My beloved Son; in Thee I am well pleased." At last God, before witnesses, declares Jesus Christ to be His Son. Satan is a liar from the beginning. It is his point when God says anything to contradict it. So the first thing he does is to say to Christ: "If Thou be the Son of God." Perhaps he wouldn't say he didn't believe it, but he was bound to dispute it. Satan started to discuss this point, and thereafter the discussion went on. [Mr. Moody—"It is going on yet."] Even when Christ went to His death, the controversy was: "If Thou be the Son of God, come down from the Cross." The people wagged their heads, saying: "Let Him save Himself now, if He be the Son of God." He was condemned on the ground of blasphemy, because He declared Himself to be the Son of God. Some people believed he was the Son of God, but the great mass did not. Yet He was attested as such by the Holy Ghost. John vi, 27: "For Him hath God the Father sealed." In the Mosaic ritual the lamb of the sacrifice was stamped and sealed by the priest as fit for the purpose. Jesus was to be offered up. The Father looked down and said: "This is My beloved Son, in whom I am well pleased. There is no spot in Him." And so the Father sealed Him. The lamb had to be eaten also. "Of this Bread if any man eat he shall not hunger." We also are sealed by the Holy Ghost. Gal. iv, 6: "Because ye are sons, God hath sent forth the Spirit of His Son into your hearts, crying Abba Father."

THE GLORIOUS MANIFESTATON.

Third: Christ was manifested. In Romans i, 3, 4, we find this remarkable statement: "Concerning His Son Jesus Christ . . . declared to be the Son of God with power, according to the spirit of holiness, by the resurrection of the dead." This was the manifestation of Christ in power. He had been in power before. When about to be crucified He declared that He could summon more than twelve legions of angels. But after His resurrection He was ready to demonstrate His Sonship. He said, "All power is given unto Me in Heaven and in earth." He was bidding them to go into all the world, and preach the Gospel unto every creature. "Who am I? One who has all power, and I am ready to use it now." He was to sit on the throne, and put Himself in communication with His disciples. To them He said, "Ye shall receive power, after that the Holy Ghost is come upon you. The works that I do shall ye do, and greater works shall ye do." "Every knee shall bow," etc. There is a wonderful truth in Romans viii, 22: "The whole creation groaneth and travaileth. . . . Even we ourselves groan within ourselves." We are going to be manifested. The sons of God will be manifested in the fullness of time. A great many went into martyrs' graves—persecuted, condemned, though the world was not worthy of them—but their day is coming. There are a great many hidden saints who are never recognized, but by-and-by they will be manifested. They will sit with Christ on His throne, sharers with Him in His power. The other day an old buried cask that had been twenty years under ground, was dug up, and thrown aside. At night a great crowd was noticed looking curiously at something. What was it? That old cask had become phosphorescent. Every stave looked as if of silver. That old rotten, decayed barrel that we threw away in the day time, at night came out luminous as the sun, in the sight of a great crowd of people. So it will be in the resurrection. In a moment the saints—given up to decay, having seen corruption—will start up from the grave to put in their glorious bodies. That will be the day of their manifestation as the sons of God. The righteous shall shine as the sun in the kingdom of the Father.

This, then, is the Three-fold Sonship. I, John iii, 2: "Beloved, now are we the sons of God; and it doth not yet appear what we shall be; but we know that when He shall be manifested (Revised Version), we shall be like Him, for we shall see Him as He is." When He is manifested, we shall be manifested. Col. iii, 3, 4: "For ye are dead, and your life is hid with Christ in God. When Christ, who is our life, shall be manifested (Revised Version), then shall we also, with Him, be manifested in glory." My heart melts within me at the wonderful grace, the wonderful elevation. It was a great condescension for Jesus Christ to become the Son of Man—born of a woman; but the greatest wonder is man being begotten of God, and being made partaker of the Divine nature. It is a great and wonderful truth that God has walked this earth; it is not a less wonderful truth that to-day there is a Man on the Throne.

FURTHER REMARKS.

The volunteer choir sang, "Beloved, Now are We the Sons of God." At Mr. Moody's instance, the hymn was repeated a few times, till all were familiar with it, and could sing it in a spirited manner. Mr. Moody then said: "I wish we had more liberty in our churches, so that when we had a subject, we could take a new hymn and practice it over and over again till we all knew it. You didn't know that hymn before, but you caught it up in five minutes. A great many people would be shocked if we did that in a church service, but it is worth while to spend five minutes that way now and then, in the regular service. It is the only time you can get the people together. We want to break up these forms, and during the service if the subject suggests a new hymn, just teach it to the people right on the spot, and send them away with it ringing in their minds. I don't know that we could have followed up Dr. Gordon's address any better than by learning that hymn. Perhaps many of you didn't take up all he said, but in the song you get the essence of it."

Mr. Geo. C. Needham referred to the responsibility attached to sonship in God. As we are like Christ in the several phases of His Sonship, so we must strive to imitate Him in our daily lives.

Dr. Pierson expatiated on the opening verses of the fourth chapter of Galatians, in which Paul shows that an heir during childhood differeth nothing from a servant though he be lord of all; but when the fullness of time is come he is recognized as a son. In Roman usages, when a son became of age, he was brought into the agora, or market-place, and there by his father publicly invested with the toga prætexta, or toga virilis (the manly toga). Sometimes also the father placed on the shoulders of the son a tunic as a mark of special favor. The people of Galatia were familiar with this custom, which afforded a beautiful illustration of the double investment of the children of God; first, in being recognized as the sons of God; and second, in being baptized by the Holy Spirit. The New Testament speaks of our Lord in seven phases: Christ prophesied, anointed, crucified, risen, ascended, glorified, and coming. In each one of these phases we share his life. But the future glory must follow a double crucifixion. We must hold the things of the world in contempt; we must submit to being held in contempt by the world. But the resurrection assures us of final triumph. Before Christ rose from the dead the grave was a dark chasm—only open on one side, the side of earth. But Jesus Christ made a hole on the other side of the grave, and turned the chasm into a tunnel; and now the light streams through from the heavenward side.

Mr. Moody said it was singular Dr. Pierson closed as he did, for at that moment the last solemn procession was marching in New York to the tomb of General Grant. He thought they should spend fifteen minutes in prayer for the bereaved family. At his request prayer was then led by the Hon. J. M. S. Williams, of Cambridge, Mass., Major Joseph Hardie, of Selma, Alabama, and Dr. Gordon.

MR. MOODY ON SINGING

In the afternoon Mr. Moody began with some further remarks about singing. He said: I got a letter since this morning saying that the Mizpah band of Glasgow, formed in 1882, is larger to-day than ever. When we were in Glasgow there were about one thousand men converted who had been slaves of strong drink, and the question was, how to hold them together. They were organized into a band, called themselves the Mizpah band, and met every Saturday. That is the time of peculiar temptation in the old countries—the men are paid off generally that day; and the week's wages generally went into whiskey. These men thought they would be tried and tempted on Saturday; so they voted that they would meet every Saturday afternoon. Then the question came up, What would bind them together? They decided that they would start a male choir. They began with a choir of four hundred; and out of those there weren't perhaps more than a dozen could sing. If you had heard them you wouldn't have thought it was singing. It sounded like old cracked kettles and tin pans. Their voices hadn't been worn down. But it kept them off the corners and out of the whiskey-shops. And they went on practicing and improving, till, in six months, when Mr. Sankey and I went back to Glasgow, I never heard such singing. They have kept on growing, and now they number over one thousand one hundred. Those men go out every week to the different parts of Glasgow, some to preach the best they know how, others to tell what God has done for them, and others to sing; and thus in one way and another, they declare the Gospel.

I mention this to bring out this fact: that a great deal of talent in all our churches lies buried. Utilize it. I think a male choir is a good thing. Let the boys get together and practice, and then use them in the churches. I think there is no singing we can have that will take hold of us more than these hymns sung by a choir like this (the male choir of the Boys'

PRIVILEGES OF BELIEVERS.

School), and they have only been practicing two or three weeks. They don't sing in an unknown tongue. In a great many churches you don't know for the life of you what they are singing about. I have been in churches where if you tried to follow the choir in your hymn book, you couldn't find the place. They might as well have sung in Greek or Latin. The music covered up the words. The mass of the people want words. They don't care about the music—it's the words. What we want is singing that will bring out the Gospel in such shape that the people won't forget it. Dr. Gordon spoke this morning on our being sons of God. and then that hymn, "Beloved, Now are We the Sons of God," came right in to clinch the sermon. I hope this question of singing will be looked into. A great many of you are representatives of churches. Do you get good music? Get the young people to sing, and in that way you will waken up a fresh interest. I believe it is easier for a man to preach after you have good live singing. I have been in churches where the choir would sing something in an unknown tongue, and then I would be too upset to preach. I would have the programme all laid out before me, but after that singing I would say to myself,"I am not fit to preach." The choir put me all out of sorts. Then I would give out "Rock of Ages," or something like that, so that everybody could sing; but the choir would find music to cover even that up. What we want is a revolution in our churches in this matter of singing. Get words and music that the people can understand. Have solos, duets, quartettes, a male choir, every kind of a choir you can get together. It is always a sign of backsliding when people don't sing. You never have a revival without singing. The nearer a man gets to God the more he wants to sing. I can't sing very well with my lips, but I can sing in my heart. I want to see new life in the singing in all our churches.

Dr. Pierson told a story of a certain choir which performed an anthem with all the ah's, and eye's and aw's. At its conclusion the minister offered the following prayer: "Oh, Lord; we suppose that Thou, being omniscient, knowest what this choir hath sung; but as for us, we have not understood one blessed word."

MR. PRATT ON GOSPEL TENT WORK.

Rev. S. H. Pratt, of Springfield, Mass., who has just closed a remarkably successful season at Pittsfield, and whose tent, "Glad Tidings," was in use on the Seminary grounds, then spoke on the advantages of tent work. He was led, he said, some time ago to consider how the summer could be utilized for God's work. Many church people, if you propose work in summer, say, "Oh, we can't do anything now. People won't come. We'll have a better chance at them in the fall or after the Week of Prayer." They really think it is presumptuous to attempt to save people in the summer time. He wanted to bear testimony to the fact that he had found God as able to save in August as in January. He commenced about eight years ago holding meetings of six, seven, or eight weeks in a city. In most of the places all the churches united. The advantages of this kind of work are:

First, A large class attend who cannot get away from home. Two-thirds of the people can't get away in summer. Why not bring some of the privileges of a convention like this to the hard-working people? In a tent they can enjoy quickening services at the end of their daily toil. Most church people like some kind of a change in summer. A good deacon said in his church there were not more than twenty-five out to prayer-meeting. Then suppose all the churches unite and have a Gospel tent during July and August? Instead of twenty-five or thirty, there will be one thousand people during the week and two thousand on Sunday night. If you get eight hundred, that eight hundred will draw five hundred more. People want to go where the people are. Instead of small, sickly prayer-meetings, you will have crowds, and a quickening influence in the community, right in the summer time.

Then, we can reach the class of people in all our cities and villages who will not come into our churches. And this class is very large. Something must be done to reach the people. A minister once said: "They can come and hear me preach. If they don't want to come let them be damned." *I* believe we ought to go to them. They are not commanded to come to the Church. The Church is commanded to go to the people. Christ said to the woman at the well that the time was coming when "neither in this mountain nor in Jerusalem" should men worship God—they were to worship Him in spirit and in truth anywhere. There is too much controversy about places to-day. Some people ask: "How do the tent converts hold out?" How do the converts in a Gothic church hold out? If a man is converted by God, he will hold out whether it is under the canvas or in a cathedral. A man born of God is a son of God, and never less than that. We are in peril of becoming formalists, and connecting our religious work with certain places. We must go anywhere—on Boston Common, as Dr. Gordon did, or on the highway. If we have prejudices against going out of church, the people we want to reach have their prejudices too, and prejudices that are well grounded. They are prejudiced against our church system. They are not prejudiced against compassion, sympathy, the pure Gospel; but they are prejudiced against our formalism and the system of running our churches. When you invite them to a free place, and just pour the compassion of the Lord Jesus Christ upon them, these prejudices are melted away. The masses are not skeptical. So far as they are they have been made skeptical by the way the work has been carried on. In New York city the class that is in the greatest need to-day is the middle class. There is a great deal of work being done for the lowest class. The neglected class to-day is the middle class—respectable men and women who earn their living and can support the Church. There are churches for the wealthy, and mission institutions for the poor; but for this respectable middle class there is no special provision made. This class can be reached.

They come by scores and hundreds to the tent in summer, and the rink or hall in winter. And one of the first evidences of their conversion is that they have a desire to join themselves with God's people. They would never want to go near a church while unconverted. One of the uses of the tent is to provide a threshold on which they can stand for a time, until they get in the right way of thinking in regard to the Church; then they can be passed on into the Church.

Another point is: We can reach Catholics in a tent. In New York the priest would tell them they must not enter a Protestant church, but never prevented them from going into the tent. So they would stand in the avenue, three or four hundred of them, listening to all the services; and then come a little nearer and nearer. Twenty or thirty gave their hearts to Christ. In Pittsfield six Catholics came out clear and strong.

By these tent services God's people are stimulated and helped all through the summer, when, perhaps, their piety shows decline. No need of lowering the standard. If you keep the standard up, you are ready to commence work in the fall. The best time for a revival, as touching the interests of a young convert, is the summer. If he is converted in the winter, the spring soon comes, Christian people leave their posts, and their is little likelihood of his getting the sympathy and care he needs. But if he is converted in the summer, he is just in time for the beginning of church work in the fall.

Mr. Moody—How much does a tent like yours cost?

Mr. Pratt—About fourteen hundred dollars. For the tent six hundred and twenty-five dollars; for the chairs six hundred and twenty-five dollars.

Mr. Moody—What does it cost to pitch it in a town for two or three weeks?

Mr. Pratt—Freight, two hundred and fifty miles, forty or fifty dollars; two dollars to light it; forty dollars a month for a man to take care of it.

Mr. Moody—I want to say it is a very good investment. There are some wealthy men here, and wealthy ladies. In the old countries it is customary for one man to take hold of one thing like this. In this country a good many wait for the Church to move. You needn't wait for the Church. Get a tent. Hire a man to preach in it all through the summer. The blessing of God rests upon such outside efforts. Then in the winter let this man go into the weak churches and preach. If he has more than he can do, hire a second man; then get a third man. I know a man who keeps three evangelists right in the field all the time? If he can find a weak church, he says to one of his men, "Here, you go to that church. I'll pay the bill." I think that is what we want in this country.

QUESTIONS AND ANSWERS.

A number of written questions were then answered by Mr. Needham, Dr. Pierson, and Dr. Gordon. Mr. Needham thought the Old Testament types ought to receive careful study. Dr. Pierson said i would be a wise rule never to draw a doctrine from a type without having first found it elsewhere; but having found it elsewhere we can take it from the type as confirmation.

Speaking of Gospel tents, Dr. Pierson said that a number of his young men in Philadelphia wanted to do some work among the masses in the summer time—they wanted to do some hot work in the summer to keep cool. They were organized into a band of about fifty, called the Evangelist Band. These young men consecrated themselves on their knees before the Lord, and now see how the Lord used them: They took a piece of ground, built around it a plain, rough board fence with a gate; then put up beams, scantlings and so on; then stretched a tent or canopy over the framework, leaving a space around where you could walk. This made a capital arrangement. These young men just put their own work in there, instead of hiring it done. For the canopy they got some old sail-cloth, at about one-third the cost of new material. After the structure was completed they whitewashed the whole interior, and made a very neat looking affair. The entire cost was only $200. When meetings were commenced the place was full every time. I don't believe, said the speaker, there has been a single service there without a conversion since it began.

PEOPLE WITH ITCHING EARS.

An important question among those answered by Dr. Pierson was this: "Should a preacher give any heed to the tastes and desires of his hearers?" Said he: No man who is a gentleman, not to say a Christian gentleman, will unnecessarily invade the preference of his hearers. There is no necessity for making yourself offensive to the tastes of other people. But with that single provision, I want to say there are two great dangers connected with the ministry in these days. One is, that they shall be afraid of the condemnation of their hearers; and another—quite as great an evil—is, that they shall be ambitious of the commendation of their people. And I don't know which is the greater. I think there is a beautiful thing in Jeremiah that I want to call attention to. Two years ago it came like a revelation to me. In the forty-second chapter of Jeremiah, the captains and leaders of the people came to the prophet, saying: "Let, we beseech thee, our supplication be accepted before thee, and pray for us unto the Lord thy God . . . . that the Lord thy God may show us the way wherein we may walk, and the thing that we may do." Jeremiah says he will do as they desire, and adds: "Whatsoever thing the Lord shall answer you, I will declare it unto you; I will keep nothing back from you." Then they reply: "The Lord be a true and faithful witness between us; if we do not even according to all things for the which the Lord thy God shall send thee to us. Whether it be good, or whether it be evil, we will obey the voice of the Lord our God." That is a most remarkable thing; and yet notice another thing: When Jeremiah got his message from God, and delivered it to them, they would not obey it, as you will see in the next chap-

PRIVILEGES OF BELIEVERS. 89

ter. They persecuted him just the moment he delivered the Lord's message to them. That is the spirit in which people are likely to look at the Cross of Jesus Christ. If a man gets his message from the study of Scripture and in prayer, he has nothing to do with what the people think or say about him. The less he knows the better, and the less he cares the better for him. In II Tim. iv, 2-4, Paul says: "Preach the Word; be instant in season, out of season; reprove, rebuke, exhort, with all long-suffering and doctrine." How much, does he say, is the preacher to think of the preferences of his hearers? "For the time will come when they will not endure sound doctrine; but after their own lusts shall they heap to themselves teachers, having itching ears." The figure here is almost too gross to be expounded. It isn't the teachers who are spoken of as having itching ears, but the hearers, and it should be so translated. They having itching ears, shall heap to themselves teachers, and turn away from the truth. Diseased animals, that have been living in the mud, find their ears itching, and they want to get a big stone or heap up something to rub their ears against. That is just what the Apostle is referring to. He says that when people get into uncleanness, and get diseased in the spiritual life, then they don't want to hear the truth, but they want to get something to relieve the itching of their ears. And so all sorts of sensationalism are resorted to, and they go where they can hear about philanthrophy, statesmanship—anything to relieve their itching ears. Now, just notice the figure still further. "They heap to themselves teachers." If a man is on the wrong track, rely upon it he will get somebody who is going to endorse his errors. Perhaps he can only find a single man in a community—for the great majority of ministers are preaching the truth; but he will go to church after church till he finds somebody to agree with him. If a man doesn't like the doctrine of future punishment, he finds some one who preaches universal salvation. He heaps up something to rub his ears against. That is why there is such a great number of false teachers; so many people having itching ears.

But a word, friends, about the danger of commendation. I hold to-day that there is nothing that is a greater snare to ministers of the Gospel than the compliments of the people to whom they preach. I venture to say that if Mr. Moody should tell you what had been to him the sorest temptation of the flesh, he would say it was the compliments that people have showered on him. I don't know how it is with other men, but the flesh is sufficiently strong in me. When a man is speaking the message of God, it comes very close to blasphemy to compliment the sermon. If you compliment the power of the sermon, you are complimenting the power of the Holy Ghost. If a minister does you good, tell him; he needs encouragement. But if there is anything that ought to humble a man, and cast him down in the dust, it is to hear some one say: "That was a splendid sermon." He has no business to preach a splendid sermon. There are occasions when a man has a right to be eloquent with secular elements;

but when he preaches the Gospel he should preach it in the power of the Holy Ghost. If he doesn't preach it in the power of the Holy Ghost it is a failure, no matter how brilliant it may be rhetorically. If he has the power of the Holy Ghost and succeeds, the best thing you can do is to say nothing, but get on your knees and ask God to bless the message. When your pastor has been the means of good to your soul, bless God.

HOW TO KNOW WE ARE SAVED.

Dr. Gordon answered the following question, among others: "I meet a good many persons who hope they are saved. Can a person *know* he is saved, and how?" Said he: The Apostle John answers that question when he says: "These things are written that ye might know." I was once obliged to meet the difficulties of a lady who was in a state of uncertainty about her salvation. She was a lady of great wealth. I said, "Do you own the house where you live?" "Yes." "Well, how do you know you own it? Is it because you feel very happy every time you walk through it?" No; that wasn't the reason. "Well; is it because the neighbors tell you you own it, and that causes you to say, with joyful feeling, 'This is really my possession?'" No; it wasn't that. "Well, then; how do you know you own the house?" "Why," said she, "if you want to know, I have the title deed to it. My husband, before he died, gave it to me; and if anybody wants to know if I own the house, I can just show that." Then I opened this passage, I

John v, 11: "This is the record, that God hath given to us eternal life, and this life is in His Son." You can't go behind the record. Do you believe? Do you accept Jesus Christ? Then how can there be any doubt about your salvation?

Mr. Moody read a letter from the London Evangelistic Committee, assuring the Convention of the sympathy and prayers of Christian friends in England.

FIRST FRUITS.

There were four sermons on Sunday—two at the forenoon and two at the afternoon service. In addition to other meetings, Dr. Gordon and Dr. Pierson preached in the forenoon; Mr. Needham and Mr. Moody in the afternoon.

DR. GORDON ON FIRST FRUITS.

Dr. Gordon took for his subject the First Fruits. He referred to seven texts, and divided his discourse under three general heads: 1. The first fruits are a specimen of the harvest. When you see them you know what the harvest will be. 2. They are an assurance of the harvest. When you see them you know the harvest is coming. 3. They are a handful of the harvest—only a diminutive part of it. (1) I Corinthians xv, 20: "Now is Christ risen from the dead, and become the first-fruits of them that slept." Christ's resurrection has shown us what our glorified body is to be. It is to be a spiritual body; but not a phantom, for the body of Christ had flesh and bones. He entered a room though the door was shut, and finally ascended into Heaven, defying the laws of gravitation, hence our glorified body will be free from the trammels of our present state. That passage: "Who shall change our vile bodies," is much better rendered in the Revised

Version. When Archbishop Whately lay dying, a brother minister read to him those words. Whately said: "No, no. The human body is a temple of the Holy Ghost. It isn't vile. Get the Greek Testament." So his friend read the verse in the Greek, and it was this: "Who shall change the body of our humiliation, and shall fashion it like the body of His glory." This body is not to be cast out because vile, but is to be changed and made glorious. Some object: "The laws of chemistry say this is impossible." I say, the laws of Scripture say it *is* possible. Chemical laws illustrate it. Take a bit of charcoal and a diamond. In substance they are precisely the same. But here is the difference: Charcoal is carbon in its humiliation; the diamond is carbon in its glory. (2) Romans viii, 21, shows that we ourselves are the first fruits of the Spirit. The harvest is coming. As yet we have only seen the first fruits. Pentecost itself was only a few drops of the coming shower. The prophecy remains to be fulfilled: "I will pour out My spirit upon all flesh," etc. When twenty thousand Telugus are converted in one of our mission fields, it is only like a man going round with a watering cart trying to make a shower. A watering cart only goes through the main streets; it doesn't go into the back alleys. But when God sends His great shower, it goes not only through the streets and avenues, but into all the back alleys. Do you hear of a great revival in Boston, New York, Philadelphia? That is only our little watering cart. When God's shower comes it will extend to all the islands of the earth.

(3) James i, 18: "Begat He us . . . . that we should be a kind of first fruits of His creatures." In the last part of the Scriptures we get a glimpse of the wonderful harvest to come. There will be chorus singing then—no small quartette singing either, but a chorus of ten thousand times ten thousand. "Hallelujah" is the only Hebrew word in the Apocalypse. This suggests that in that great chorus of the redeemed the Jews are included; they have been gathered in, and while the vast hosts are singing, they, now and then, in a deep bass voice, break in with the shout, "Hallelujah!" Once the Jews cried, "Not this man, but Barabbas." They chose a murderer and robber, and how they have been murdered and robbed all down the ages! They chose Cæsar as king, and how Cæsars have oppressed them ever since! But when the times of the Gentiles are fulfilled, they are to look on Him whom they have pierced, and reverse their cry, saying, "Not Barabbas, but this Man." (4) Romans xi, 16: "For if the first-fruit be holy, the lump is also holy." (5) 1 Cor. xvi, 15: "The first-fruits of Achaia"—in other words, the first-fruits of missions in Asia. In this latter half of the nineteenth century we are seeing something of the harvest, in Asia especially. (6) Rom. xvi, 5: Another reference to the first-fruits in Achaia. (7) "These are they which follow the Lamb whithersoever He goeth. These were redeemed from among men, being the first-fruits unto God and the Lamb." May the Lord prepare us! May we have a solemn sense of personal responsibility as Christians, so to live as to be ready for His coming!

DR. PIERSON ON CHRIST IN THE OLD TESTAMENT.

Dr. Pierson read Luke xxiv, 27: "Beginning at Moses, and all the prophets, He expounded unto them in all the Scriptures the things concerning Himself." Again, verse 44: "He said unto them, These are the words which I spake unto you, while I was yet with you, that all things must be fulfilled, which were written in the law of Moses, and in the prophets, and in the Psalms, concerning Me." The Jews divided their Scriptures into three portions: the law, the prophets, and the Psalms. These words of Christ, therefore, were equivalent to saying that the entire Old Testament was full of references to Him. There is but one book, the Bible. There is but one person, the Lord Jesus Christ. Richard Porson, the Shakesperian scholar, was so familiar with the words of his master that it is said he could hold a conversation for three days, and express all his ideas in the dialect of Shakespeare. Is it not a greater wonder that 1,800 years after our Master has ascended into glory, we can hold a convention for ten days, and speak only the dialect of our Lord Jesus Christ? It is true that all throughout the Old Testament Scriptures, everywhere you can find Christ. In the first place, in the prophetic Scriptures there are distinct and definite prophecies concerning His coming, humiliation, death and resurrection. In the second place, we find Jesus Christ in the types. He is revealed in the sacrificial ceremonies. In the third place, we find Him revealed in the allegorical portions of Scripture; for we are told that the historical portions have an allegorical meaning. Paul says regarding Hagar and Ishmael, "which things are an allegory." In the fourth place, we find Christ in the enigmas of Scripture. Apparent contradictions are only reconciled by the blood of Jesus Christ. I shall only have time to speak of the prophetic and the typical Scriptures. Why was there an interval of 400 years between the close of the Old Testament and the coming of Christ? It was in order to show that there could have been no contact or collusion between the prophets of the Old Testament and the Evangelists of the New. Suppose you are traveling in a foreign country, and are called upon to unlock the door of a certain closet in some mysterious castle. You try and fail. You send for the best locksmiths, and they fail. But, while you continue your travels, you find in another castle 500 or 1,000 miles away, a key which you think, from the character of its wards, is just what you wanted. You hasten back, and put it in the lock; instantly the bolts are flung back, and you open the door. At once you conclude that the same man must have made both the lock and the key. Precisely so is it when we find that, notwithstanding a separation of 400 years, Jesus Christ is the fulfillment of prophecy. How many of us have ever looked into the argument from simple and compound probability? If I utter a prophecy that contains a certain particular, there will be a chance of a fulfillment and a chance of its non-fulfillment. It will be a wonder if it is fulfilled, yet there is half a chance that it will be. Suppose I utter a prediction containing two particulars: I add another element; the half-chance must be divided, and there is only left a quarter of a chance. If you get twenty-five particulars in a prophecy, all of which must unite in the fulfillment, you have got to raise one-half to its twenty-fifth power in order to estimate the probability of such a thing occurring. And when you bring one-half to its twenty-fifth power, you get into millions and billions. You must have one chance against millions and billions of chances in order that the thing shall occur. This shows the magnificent power of the argument from prophecy. It never has been met—never will be met. Not only do the prophetic Scriptures contain direct predictions concerning Christ, but the whole Bible is full of indirect allusions to Him, and the salvation He came to achieve. Something about this great salvation is literally contained in every book of the Bible from Genesis to Malachi. Dr. Pierson then reviewed every book of the Old Testament to prove this statement and to exhibit the wonderful wealth of the Hebrew Scriptures in types prefiguring Christ. He closed with an impressive application, warning hearers that should any still be rejecting the Saviour, all those voices would be raised against them, and leave them without excuse before the bar of God.

MR. NEEDHAM ON THE PRIESTHOOD OF CHRIST.

Mr. George C. Needham spoke in the afternoon on "The Priesthood of Christ," taking as his text Hebrews iv, 14: "Seeing then that we have a great high priest, that is passed into the heavens,

Jesus the Son of God, let us hold fast our profession." He likened the present ministry of Christ to the rainbow, that glorious arch which leaves the earth at one point to return to it at another. Christ's ministry runs parallel with the ministry of the Spirit; His intercession is for us; the intercession of the Spirit is *in* us. 1. The certainty of His priestly ministry for us. The statements of Christianity are absolute. "We *have* a great high priest." It is our privilege to know the fact. There may be agnostics outside of Christianity, but a Christian agnostic is inconceivable. The basis of our knowledge is the Word of God, and we have only to adapt our conduct to the truth it reveals, Heb. iii, 1: "Consider the apostles and High Priest of our profession, Christ Jesus." 2. The necessity of Christ's priesthood. In some form priesthood is recognized in nearly all religions. Man's cry is (Job ix, 33): "Neither is there any daysmen betwixt us, that might lay his hand upon us both!" God's answer is (1 Tim. ii, 5): "This is good and acceptable in the sight of God our Saviour, who will have all men to be saved . . . For there is one God, and one Mediator between God and men, the man Christ Jesus." He is the "God-man"—from man to God. The title "priest" signifies a sacrificer. It implies the offering of a victim to God and certain results flowing therefrom. Priesthood is a necessity (Heb. vii, 3). 3. Qualifications. Under the Jewish law certain requirements were demanded. The priest must be without blemish (Lev. 17, 18, 21.) Christ was holy, harmless, undefiled, separate from sinners (Heb. vii, 26). He must be human, in order that he may be humane—compassionate (Heb. v, 1, 2). He must be of Divine appointment (Heb. v, 4). The right of Christ to the priesthood stands unchallenged. His priesthood began in His resurrection. "Touch Me not," He said; "I ascend." He must be in the married state, with a spotless wife (Lev. xxi, 13, 14.) The bride of Christ is the Church (2 Cor. xi, 2; Rev. xix, 7, 8). 4. The place of priestly ministry. The priests of old officiated in the tabernacle and the Temple. The holy and most holy places were shadows of realities to come. Christ hath ascended into Heaven, where His priesthood is exercised (Heb. iv, 14; viii, 1, 2; x, 11, 12.) We see Him standing to receive Stephen. 5. The design of the priesthood. This is, first, to present atonement for sin (Lev. xvi, 15, 21, 22; Heb. ix, 14-26), and to affect reconciliation. Secondly, to present worship and the worshipper acceptably to God (John xiv, 23; Eph. v, 2; Rev. viii, 3, 4; Col. i, 21, 22; Jude 24). The priesthood, further, is the medium of blessing (Num. vi, 22-27; Luke xxiv, 50, 51). 6. Three parts of the priestly ministry. Christ is our Advocate (1 John ii, 1); our Intercessor (Heb. vii, 24, 25); our Keeper (John xvii); and our Mediator—the Bridge, the Way.

SERMON BY MR. MOODY.

Mr. Moody then preached a sermon, which was listened to eagerly throughout by the one thousand five hundred persons present. It was addressed chiefly to the unconverted. For want of space here, it will be published in full in an early number of *Sabbath Reading*, in which form it will be specially well adapted for distribution. The following will serve as a synopsis: Mr. Moody took as his subject the grace of God, and as his text, Titus ii, 11-15: "For the grace of God that bringeth salvation hath appeared to all men," etc. Said he: "I like to preach the Gospel—it's so free. A great many people lose salvation because they think they can attain it by good works. To secure salvation, all that we have to do is to believe in Christ. Good works come after salvation, not before it. When Christ has offered His own body as an atonement for sin, let us not insult Him by offering anything in ourselves for the same purpose. Some men are fond of boasting that they are "self-made." There will be none of that kind of boasting in Heaven. A Southern spy heaped all manner of curses on Lincoln's head, till he was pardoned; then, overcome by the president's magnanimity, he became his warmest friend and defender. That is a faint picture of God's grace. "Every mouth shall be stopped." God will allow no flesh to boast in His presence. If we want salvation we must take it as a gift. Think what this salvation means. It is life—life eternal. If I offered this audience a $10,000 bill, all the sheriffs in this county couldn't keep back the crowd that would come tumbling over these seats. And yet you won't take eternal life.

We must have good works, it is true, but they are the result of salvation. Man works *from* the Cross. Some people take that verse, " Work out your own salvation with fear and trembling;" and think that means they are to get salvation by working it out. But this text is only for those who already have salvation. How are you going to work out your salvation until you have it? God gives us grace enough to work out our salvation as we go along. Remember, He won't give it to us all at once. If He did we wouldn't know what to do with it. A man once built a house on the shore of Lake Erie, and laid a pipe from the lake to supply the house with water. Suppose some one had given him the whole lake. What could he have done with it? He only wanted communication with the lake. God supplies us with just as much grace as we need, and no more. Don't be afraid you won't get all you require. I was once talking with an English woman on this subject. She was afraid she couldn't live a Christian life, because there would be so many trials and temptations in future. I tried in one way and another to convince her that she need have no misgivings—that God would supply daily grace sufficient for every emergency. Nothing availed till I used the old story of the clock. The pendulum of a clock once became discouraged—didn't see how it was ever going to tick out all the hours it was expected to measure. The clock reasoned with it, saying, "Only one tick at a time," and so it went on with its slow and steady "tick-tick." The lady caught the idea, and talked so much about that clock that people called her Lady Pendulum. She sent me a beautiful clock, that's now ticking away over at my house. The Lord will always give us grace as we ask for it—

enough for the time. There ought to be no room, then, for the devil, if our hearts are full of this grace. For the Christian there is peace in the past, hope in the present, and glory in the future. Child of God, lift up your head. Soon will come that glory. When a Christian dies, it is like the sowing of corn —only sown for a life. It is a mistake to talk about the "dark valley of the shadow of death." It isn't dark. If it was there couldn't be any shadow. Did you ever see a shadow in a dark cellar? There must be light to make a shadow, and there is light even in the valley of death. God's grace is for all. We shall have all we need if we only keep near the base of supply. We will have trials and temptations; but thorns in the flesh are a good thing for us. Paul's prison showed how we ought to sing in tribulation. The devil thought he had put an end to John Bunyan when he got him into Bedford jail, but it was there he wrote the "Pilgrim's Progress." A good many people want grace to die by. What we need is grace to live by. If we have that, God will give us dying grace.

We must use grace to work out our salvation. The grace of God will make us kind, true, honest, upright. If it doesn't do that for me I don't want it. The Church of God should seek to live on a higher plane. If Christians would exhibit more of God's grace in their daily lives they could meet the world better. We want more "peculiar" people. No doubt Enoch was considered peculiar by the public of his day. He wouldn't have gone to a horserace. He was peculiar, but he walked with God, and one day he was taken up to Heaven without dying. Gone for a long walk, isn't he? Elijah was considered peculiar—people thought him very conceited and bigoted. But he was right and the world was wrong; and God honored him by taking him up in a chariot of fire. Paul, at Rome, seemed a fanatic, a madman; but what Roman orator, general, or emperor has his fame? "Be zealous of good works." This morning I found on my breakfast plate this text: "Zealous of Good Works," from Lady Pemberton, of London—done in dried flowers from her own garden. She is confined to her room, a cripple, but she has made two hundred and fifty of these with her own hands and sent them to the London hospitals. People talk about having zeal without knowledge. I'd rather have zeal without knowledge than knowledge without zeal. Go to work. Let God use you. If he could use an old dried-up rod in the hands of Moses, can't He use you? If He could use those old ram's horns before Jericho, or the jawbone of an ass in the hand of Samson, or the little stone in the sling of David, can't He use you? Be zealous of good works. Be used of God. Whatever is done for God cannot be small. When the widow put her mite in the box at the Temple, if there were any Jerusalem reporters picking up items, they wouldn't have thought that worthy of a paragraph; but they would have been sure to tell about the rich Mrs. Levi and her gift of $1,000, to the extent of half-a-column with big headlines. Yet the smaller gift was the larger. Everyone has heard about the widow's mite; and mite societies must have brought in millions of dollars to the Church. The trouble is, too many men sneak behind the widow's mite. A rich man to whom I once applied for a contribution, said, while handing me a dollar, "Well, I will give the widow's mite." "Will you," said I, "then I'll take all you've got. That's what she gave." Despise not the day of small things. Mary's memorial is known around the earth to-day. "She hath done what she could."

DR. PIERSON ON MISSIONS.

In the afternoon a stirring address was made by Dr. Pierson on the subject of missions. Said he: Evangelization is universal. It consists in preaching, teaching, and testifying. It relies on three promises of Christ: to be always with us, to send the Holy Spirit, and to give supernatural signs. It is obligatory, and not only upon ministers or missionaries, but upon all. Christlieb says: "The modern era of foreign missions is the closest parallel of the supernatural signs of old that we have in the recurrence of events in present time." The miracle of regeneration among abandoned men is God's pillar of fire to-day. See how obstacles have been removed. These obstacles fell into four groups: of approach, of intercourse, of impression, and of action. Glance at the way these were combined and the wonderful manner in which they have melted away. When the work began, the penetration of the continents with the Gospel was a physical impossibility. Many nations of the earth were shut even to commerce. China was enclosed by the sea and the great wall.

Africa was a vast stretch of unexplored country—only the mere thread of coast-line being known geographically. The deeds of the Fiji Islanders to missionaries had been fiendish, horrible beyond expression, written in blood and registered in hell. Languages in scores were unknown, without grammar or dictionary. Women in thousands, cooped up in zenana, harem, and seraglio, were absolutely inaccessible. Now every country has been opened up. Even Corea, the hermit nation, has been opened up. Over twenty thousand women in foreign lands can be reached by the Gospel. Sixty languages have been reduced to writing and a grammatical form. Not one obstacle out of fifty that confronted us at the beginning impedes us now.

All this has been accomplished by devoted labor. William Johnson, who died in Sierra Leone, after seven years' work, left every trade, industry, and profession interested, with a church of a capacity of one thousand six hundred, whereas, at his coming, more than twenty kinds of people were living with a miserable little sign language. In India, in 1868, there was wrought the most magnificent work since the day of Pentecost. I tell you the Gospel is done with traveling by stage coach. It goes by lightning. History gives glorious testimony to the spreading of the Word among men. At the opening of the eighteenth century the air was full of deism, atheism, and lasciviousness. Louis XVI and Mme. de Pompadour were at the head of France; with Frederick the Great under the influence of Voltaire, Germany was tumbling under an influx of rationalism and skepticism. Then God sent out the twelve modern apostles, with Whitefield and Wesley at their head. With the year 1747 opens the era of modern missions, when Jonathan Edwards sent out from Northampton a tract asking for the effusion of the Spirit upon the habitable globe—a trumpet peal to the whole world. In 1757 occurred the battle of Plassy, when Lord Clive, sword in hand, gave England the entering wedge to India. In 1792 the first missionary society was organized. William Carey, the "consecrated cobbler," was sent out to India from England. In the fourteen years succeeding to the first, seven foreign missions were founded. Commodore Perry entered Japan in 1853; in 1857 occurred the Sepoy mutiny, which gave new impulse to the Indian work, showing the natives what friends they had in the English. In 1858, England, France and America concluded the treaty with China, which added thirty-five million more to the missionary effort. The year 1868 was the *annus mirabilus* in evangelical work, no fewer than ten thousand people being baptized in one week and sixty thousand during the winter, while twenty individuals alone gave $4,000,000 for mission work. In 1873 Turkey joined the lands open to work. In 1873 Stanley, as a reporter of the New York *Herald*, went after Livingston, finding him in 1877, fulfilling the prophecy in regard to Ethiopia. In one thousand days after his return the Congo chain of lakes was compassed; in one thousand more there was a chain of stations along them. In 1884, as a result of the Berlin conference, the

Congo state was established, civil and reilgious liberty being assured, not only Protestant nations such as England, and Catholic such as Italy, but the Greek Church of Russia, and the Moslem, agreeing to the compact.

Now, said the speaker, what shall be the practical outcome of this Convention? What is wanted is a World's Conference. Let witnesses come from all parts of the world to tell what the Lord is doing, so that we may light upon the altars of our hearts new consecrated fires. Let the missionary societies of all the denominations take part, and let them agree to follow principles of courtesy and comity, so that wherever one denomination has a successful work, other denominations will not interfere, but look farther, and go into the destitute places. At this great council let it be resolved that there shall not be one portion of the earth without some responsible Christian denomination to take charge of its evangelists. Let the missionaries multiply. Let them be not only educated clergymen, accustomed to intellectual employment—contact with books; but let them be taken from every walk of life, and thrust into contact with men. Let these young men and young women go through short courses of training in the history of missions, and in the knowledge of the Word of God and Christian doctrine. Then let them go into those great fields, and continue their studies, not in Greek, Latin and Hebrew, but in the language of the very heathen among whom they labor. While they are getting acquainted with the people and the language, let them do such work as they can in connection with the mission—setting type, etc., or even menial labor. Such young men and women will do splendid work for the Master.

POWER—PENTECOST POSSIBLE IN THE NINETEENTH CENTURY.

SECRET OF SUCCESS.

THE GIFT OF THE HOLY SPIRIT FOR SERVICE—ADDRESSES BY MR. MOODY AND OTHERS—VARIOUS PRACTICAL HINTS.

Rev. Dr. Gordon spoke on the Holy Spirit, taking as his text John xiv, 16, 17. He called special attention to the change in the tense: "Ye know Him; for He dwelleth (present tense) with you, and shall be (future tense) in you." Before the day of Pentecost God dwelt *with* His people; after it He dwelt *in* His people. In Old Testament times a cloud of glory hung over the Mercy-Seat. The Jews have a curious tradition. They say that when God finally became weary of the apostacy of Israel, this cloud lifted from the Mercy-Seat and remained for three-and-a-half years on the top of Mount Olivet, during which time a voice could be heard saying, "Seek ye the Lord while He may be found; call ye upon Him while He is near." At last the cloud lifted from the brow of Olivet, went away to Heaven, and was seen no more. This cloud came back in the person of

Jesus Christ. He was the temple of flesh, dedicated on the banks of the Jordan; and in Him God dwelt. Again for three-and-a-half years God pleaded with Israel; and when Christ ascended the cloud rose and departed the second time. The third temple consists of the hearts of believers. See how it was dedicated. The disciples were gatherd with one accord in one place. Suddenly the Holy Ghost descended upon them with tongues of fire, and sat upon each of them. Notice that word "sat"—it is significant. Just as the cloud sat upon the Mercy-Seat, the Holy Ghost descended in visible form and "sat upon each of them." Immediately the Holy Ghost was spoken of as the present authority. Ananias and Sapphira were punished because they had "lied unto the Holy Ghost." The Apostle said, " It seeemed good to the Holy Ghost and to us."

This wonderful truth—of the indwelling of the Spirit—is the characteristic trait of the dispensation in which we live. If whatever is true of Christ is true of us, it will repay us to examine the account of His baptism. (Luke iv.) In it we find four things: He was filled with the Spirit; was led by the Spirit; had the power of the Spirit; and was anointed by the Spirit.

"FILLED."

1. The first thing said of the disciples after Pentecost was that they were "filled with the Holy Ghost." Whenever there was anything important to be done, it says, for example: "Paul, being filled with the Spirit," spake thus: "Peter, being filled with the Spirit," did this. It was characteristic of

the Apostolic Church that they were men full of the Holy Ghost. Is that our privilege? It is not only our privilege; it is our duty. "Be filled with the Spirit," is a command. "Be not drunken with wine, wherein is excess; but be filled with the Spirit, speaking unto one another in psalms and hymns, and spiritual songs." If a man is drunk with wine he will speak out. He won't have to be educated before he will let loose his tongue. If a man is filled with the Holy Spirit he won't have to learn much before he can deliver his message—it will come spontaneously. In Germany, a man was once so holy that the neighbors called him the "God-intoxicated man." We want a "God-intoxicated Church." Some one says: "That is a great mystery. How can we be filled with the Spirit?" Well, we can't fill ourselves. But there is one thing we can do; we can empty ourselves. In speaking of the Spirit, Christ uses the simile of the wind. You know the wind always blows towards a vacuum. If we can make a vacuum in our hearts, the Holy Ghost will fill them. During that ten days before Pentecost, do you suppose the disciples were just praying over and over again? I think they did a good deal more than pray. I imagine they were just emptying their hearts. Peter says: "I am headstrong and rash. I wanted to call down fire from heaven. I denied my Master." They were confessing their faults while waiting for power. In ten days they had got their hearts really empty, when the Spirit came like a rushing, mighty wind, to fill the vacuum. I wonder how many of you have read the life of James Brainerd Taylor. He was a graduate of Princeton, and only twenty-eight when he died; yet he did a work that any man might envy. He got hold of the idea that there was something in this doctrine of the enduement of the Spirit. Studying the subject, he became perfectly sure that the Holy Ghost might come upon him as upon the original disciples. So he prayed, and his prayers were answered. Whenever he went out he stirred all with whom he came in contact. Sinners used to fall before his preaching as grass before the scythe. It was spontaneous. He couldn't help speaking to men; and his words were mighty. There is one very beautiful incident in his life. One day he was out driving, and he drew his horse up to a watering-trough. It so happened that another young man was doing the same thing. While the two horses' heads met in the trough, he turned to the young man and said: "I hope you love the Lord. If you don't, I want to commend him to you as your best friend. Seek Him with all your heart." That was all; they turned and went their ways. But what was the result? The young man thus spoken to was converted, was educated for the ministry, and went as a missionary to Africa. Said this missionary afterwards: "Over and over again I wished I knew who that man was who spoke to me at the watering-trough. But I never knew, till some one sent to me in Africa a box of books. I opened them; saw a little black-covered book; opened it; turned to the title page, and there I saw a portrait—a beautiful face. 'Ah,' said I, 'that is the man. That's the man who preached the Gospel to me at the watering-trough. To him I owe my salvation.'" And that of how many more on the Dark Continent? What we want to-day is to be filled with the Spirit. We are filled with so many other things—pride, selfishness, ambition, and vain-glory. May the Lord enable us to empty our hearts, and have them filled as with a mighty rushing wind!

"LED."

2. Christ was led by the Spirit. Believers are thus led. Leading implies going before. One hymn I criticise: "Holy Spirit, faithful Guide, ever near the Christian's side." The Spirit is not beside us; He goes before to lead. Some people ask whether it is possible to be led by the Spirit as in the days of old. I believe it is. When the Spirit told Philip to join himself to the eunuch, He touched both Philip and the eunuch at the same time—struck two notes, producing perfect harmony. Does not the same thing occur in our own experience? One morning my wife said to me, "I must go and talk with so-and-so, mentioning a young man's name. This young man was the son of a wealthy father, and had been reared in most aristocratic circumstances, but had proven a profligate, and had been turned out of the house. We did not know him especially, but my wife had an overwhelming impression that she must go and speak to him. As soon as she got her breakfast, we prayed together that the Lord would use the word, and she started off. She got to the house, rang the bell, was admitted, and the young man was called. When he came into the

room he said, "I am glad you have come to see me," and it wasn't half an hour till he was on his knees. The Spirit had prepared his heart, and then caused my wife to go and see him. He is now a sober, steadfast Christian young man. Thomas Guthrie says that one day when he was out walking there came to him a most curious, irresistible impulse to go and see a widow who lived in a cottage in that vicinity. Says he: "I had been to see her recently, and didn't think it was necessary to go again so soon. But the impression came with such tremendous force that I started on a run. On the way I met one of my most intimate friends, who wanted to talk with me. 'I can't stop,' I said; 'I am in a great hurry.' On I ran with all my might, till I got to this widow's cottage. She was a helpless cripple—had been left alone—the servant had gone out and the house was on fire! When I got there the flames were on either side of her, sweeping nearer and nearer. Had I been five minutes too late she must have perished. I lifted her in my arms, and took her out of the house." Now, don't you believe the Spirit of God told Thomas Guthrie to go to that cottage just as truly as He told Philip to go to the chariot of the eunuch? I think if we were led by the Spirit we would have a great deal more freedom about everything. "Where the Spirit of the Lord is, there is liberty." Some people think that it means liberty for them to do just about as they please. The real meaning is very different. The Spirit is to do just as *He* pleases. I never shall forget how I was startled when a young man—a stranger, but a very good Christian man—asked this question: "Do you always have a programme made out for the Holy Ghost in your church?" That was all he asked; but it stuck to me. Everything was fixed very exactly—a voluntary here, a response here, a sermon here, and so on—all fixed from beginning to end. I don't think the Spirit of God has anything to do with that. Let us have more liberty. It is the lack of this liberty that causes so much deadness in the pulpit, and deadness in the pew. Oh, for the liberty of the Spirit!

IN THE SPIRIT'S POWER.

3. The Lord went in the power of the Spirit. His final words to His disciples were: "Ye shall receive power, after that the Holy Ghost is come upon you." It is a remarkable fact that in Scripture there are fifty-two passages in which "power" and "Holy Ghost" are linked together. Water assumes three different shapes: ice, liquid, and vapor. It is the vapor, though invisible, which moves the machinery of this nineteenth century. Of the three persons in the God-head, perhaps the Holy Spirit receives least attention from us. Yet it is the power of the Spirit that propels the machinery of all our missionary efforts. Oh, for this power! David Brainerd went often into the woods to wrestle with God in prayer, and, sometimes, though the weather was cold, he would remain till every thread of his clothing was wet with the sweat of his intercession. Every such period of prayer was immediately followed by a great outpouring of the Spirit.

"ANOINTED."

4. Christ was anointed. There were two parts of the anointing ceremony—the sprinkling of blood, and anointing with oil. One was the symbol of cleansing, the other of sanctifying. After we are regenerated something remains to be done. We must be sanctified. When a leper was cleansed, the priest anointed with oil the tip of his right ear, the thumb of his right hand, and the great toe of his right foot. This signifies that we are to be thoroughly sanctified in every part of our being. Every part of our body is to be used for God. Do you say, "I am not ordained to be a preacher." Well, perhaps you are a good singer. God holds you to do something. When the people of a church become thoroughly consecrated, a revival is sure to follow. Once the great Athenian general, Themistocles, was about to fight a naval battle. All were ready when the sun rose, but the order to advance did not come. Hour after hour passed—no command to advance. Some of the officers murmured, saying: "Is Themistocles afraid? Is he a traitor? or is he going to fight that battle?" But Themistocles knew what he was about. According to the geography of that country, at nine o'clock a land breeze sweeps down from the mountain. He thought: "Now, if I wait till nine o'clock, instead of having half of my men at the oars and the other half at the spears, I can let the wind do the business." So he waited; the wind filled the sails; and he won the battle, because every man was a warrior. That is what we want—every man a warrior. In our churches there are too many men at

the oars. There is a committee on music—three or four men to attend to the music, and that is all they have to do year in and year out. Then we have a committee on credentials, and a committee on finances, and a committee to attend to the social interests of the young people. And thus our churches are all divided up into committees, so that when we come to the great work to be done—the conversion of souls—our men are all engaged at the oars. Oh, that we might understand that it is possible to have this heavenly breeze, to fill our sails, and release us from the oars. Let our motto be, "Every man a warrior!"

THE GIFT OF THE HOLY SPIRIT.

ADDRESS BY MR. MOODY.

By special request, Mr. Moody spoke on "The Gift of the Holy Spirit for Service." Said he: I want to call attention to the work of the Spirit. Now, the first thing the Holy Ghost does with a man—an unconverted man—is to convince him of sin. No other power can convince a man of sin but the power of the Holy Ghost. I believe you might fill this building with unconverted people, and then, if you could, you might even get the angel Gabriel to come down here and preach to them, and if he were to preach without the Holy Ghost there wouldn't be one soul converted. If an angel from Heaven hasn't got the power of the Holy Ghost, he cannot convict of sin. I would rather give up the work I am engaged in—I would rather go and break stones or saw wood than do the work I am engaged in if I had to convince an audience of sin. It is a very comforting thought that that is not my work. My work is to declare the truth; it is the work of the Holy Spirit to convince of sin.

LOVE OF GOD.

Then, after a man has been convinced of sin, and is willing to give up his sins—for unless a man is willing to give up his sins, there is no chance for God to save him—when he is willing to give up his sins and ask God for mercy, the next act of the Holy Ghost is to shed abroad the love of God in that man's heart. You might as well tell me that you can leap over the Atlantic Ocean or fell an American forest with a penknife, as to say you can love God with the natural heart. No unregenerate heart can love God. When a man is born of God, and has become a partaker of the Divine nature, then comes this second thing, to love God; and that is the work of the Holy Ghost—to impart or shed abroad the love of God in our hearts. Love is spontaneous. You can't make yourself love. The moment the Spirit of God gives you the power, you can't help loving Him. In Galatians v, 22, Paul says the fruit of the Spirit is love, joy, peace, long-suffering, gentleness, goodness, faith, etc. But these are all summed up in love. Joy is only love exalted. Faith is only love in the battlefield. So you can sum up every one of these qualities, and they all come to one word at last. And if a man is full of love, the first thing you see he is at work for God. He has got done talking about duty. He has risen into a higher plane. The love of God constrains him, so that he can't help but work—it is his delight to work.

HOPE.

The next thing the Holy Ghost does is: It imparts hope. You never saw a discouraged man in your life who was full of the Holy Ghost. You never saw a man full of the Holy Spirit going around with his head down. A man full of the Holy Ghost is a hopeful man. He knows the time is coming when Christ will appear in His kingdom, and his scepter will sway the whole earth. We want to be full of hope. Let a minister become discouraged, and it will be like a contagious disease in his congregation. I have known ministers to be discouraged—disheartened. When they are in that condition, if they will take my advice, they will get out of the pulpit. They are doing more harm than good. God never will use a man when he has lost courage. Look at Elijah—cast out of the community. There he was, cast down, no better than his fathers. That is just the position of a good many of God's children; they have lost hope, become discouraged. A physician told me that a friend of his came to him greatly cast down, greatly depressed. Said he: "I said to this man: 'Have you any doubt that it is the decree of high Heaven that every knee shall bow and every tongue confess Christ?' 'Well,' the man said, 'Christ will come and reign over the whole earth!' 'Do you believe it? Then what are you cast down for?'" We needn't be cast down. It is only a question of time before the stone cut out of the mountain is going to become like a great mountain and fill the whole earth. Christ shall reign. If He is going to reign, you and I ought to be full of hope. There was a minister in Glasgow who had no hope at all. Some one said to him, "You will accept results, won't you?" "Oh, yes; I will accept results." "Well, here is the Bible; you can see what Christ is going to do. If the Bible says it is going to be done, it is just as good as done, isn't it?" A minister without hope can do his people no good. A Sabbath-school teacher, discouraged, disheartened, can do the children no good. They know very well that their teacher is good for nothing. Therefore it is very important we have hope; and if we have the Spirit, we have hope.

LIBERTY.

The next thing: We have liberty. I believe a man who is full of the Holy Ghost will have liberty. What we want in our churches more than anything else is this liberty. Why, look at the stiffness in most of our churches. Put a man in an audience where men and women are going to criticise, and he won't have much liberty—much freedom. In the day of Pentecost, how many do you suppose criticised? I don't believe Peter would have preached near as well as he preached if the people had been criticising him. Suppose those Jews had been full of criticism, I don't believe a soul would have been converted. But while Peter was preaching the people were listening in a proper frame of mind, and they helped him right on. He just had liberty that day—great liberty. When you see a minister in the pulpit who doesn't have liberty, pray for him. You will find he will get on much better than if you were to sit there and criticise him. When a man has the Spirit in him, he will have liberty. It won't be hard for him to speak. It won't be hard for him to testify. There's many a man toiling—working hard in the pulpit, and no liberty—seeming to be bound hand and foot. Ah, my friends, where the Spirit of the Lord is, there will be liberty.

TESTIFYING OF CHRIST.

The next thing the Spirit does—it testifies of Christ. That is His work, to testify of Christ. "He shall not speak of Himself." "He shall testify of Me." On the day of Pentecost the Spirit did testify of Christ. Peter, under the power of the Holy Ghost, spoke of Christ all through his sermon, and ended it by saying: "God hath made that same Jesus, whom ye have crucified, both Lord and Christ." That same Jesus they had crucified, God had taken up out of Joseph's sepulchre, and seated Him at His own right hand. Peter told the Jews this great truth, and the Holy Ghost said, "Amen." Now, if the Holy Ghost hadn't given Peter freedom, he might have preached for ten years and there wouldn't have been a soul converted—the people wouldn't have believed; but the Holy Ghost bore witness as Jesus said He would do. Go into your pulpit, or Sabbath-school class, and though you may declare the truth, if the Spirit doesn't testify to what you say, it will be just beating against the air, and there will be no power.

A TEACHER.

Another thing He will do: He will teach you all things. I like that word—*all* things. He will teach us all things that it is best for us to know. I think it is very dishonoring to God to go around trying to learn the things He has hidden from us in any other way than the way He has provided. We have got the Holy Ghost. He has been sent down from Heaven to guide us into all truth. He will teach us all things, and show us the things of God. So I believe it is very dishonoring for us to be running off after departed spirits when we have got the Holy Spirit. Honor Him. Let Him be your Guide. "He shall guide you into all truth." The Holy Ghost never led a man into darkness, or error, or superstition. He leads him into the full blaze of Calvary. "He will guide you into all truth . . . and He will show you things to come." A lot of people have got an idea now that this old Book is worn out, and that when we preach from the Bible we are only harping on the same old thing. Why, here is a Book that will tell you the future. Where can you get anything fresher than you have got here? If I wanted to know the future I wouldn't go to the Springfield *Republican*. The best that newspapers can do is to tell you what *has* happened. This Book tells you what is going to happen. Do you want to know what is going to happen thousands of years hence? This is the only book in the world that will tell you. What it said thousands of years ago would happen is coming to pass now, and what it says will take place in the future is just as certain. It is absurd to talk about this Book having lost its power. I'd like to see some of these philosophers building a house with no windows in it. Why don't they build a house without any windows, and say, "We have got the electric light now, we can shut out the sun. That's old!" Would that be sensible? Yet there would be just as much sense in that as there is in talking the same way about this old Book.

A COMFORTER.

Then, the Holy Spirit is a Comforter. "He will comfort you." When Christ was crucified, His disciples seemed to have forgotten all He had ever said to them. He had told them over and over again that He would rise again on the third day. His enemies remembered that. They had better memories than His disciples, for they set soldiers to watch His grave. It has always been a mystery to me why every disciple of Christ was not around that sepulchre waiting. He had told them He would rise; but they wouldn't believe it, or they seemed to forget. But after the day of Pentecost, then it was that all the words of Christ came bubbling up in their souls. They were just filled with the words of the Lord Jesus. What made the difference? It was the Holy Spirit. "But the Comforter, which is the Holy Ghost, whom the Father will send in My name, He shall teach you all things, and bring all things to your remembrance, whatsoever I have said unto you." Yes, He will cause you to remember what the Lord Jesus has said. My friends, isn't that your experience? When the Spirit comes upon you, the dew of heaven flashes upon you like a light, and you see things in a new beauty. He shall comfort you —bring passages to your minds. Look at the bed-ridden ones—the afflicted ones. Oh, what comfort they have in the truths brought to their remembrance by the Holy Ghost.

THE ANCIENT TEMPLE.

Now, I want to call your attention to three dwelling places the Holy Spirit has on this earth. In the tabernacle of Moses I read that they made a place for God to come, and he came in the form of the Shekinah cloud. The cloud filled the tabernacle, and Moses was not able to enter the tent. I suppose some in this audience have had that experience. God has so filled them with His Spirit that they have had to cry, "Stay Thine hand." I have no doubt that this was Moses' experience. That tabernacle was so filled with the glory of God that he couldn't endure it. And then I read again that when the Temple was built, the Levites were all with one accord in the house, and formed a choir. There was no quarreling among the singers there. You know lots of churches are troubled with wrangling among the singers. I don't see how they can sing at all when they are in that condition. If they can't keep their hearts warm with the love of God, they can't sing the praises of God. The Levites were all with one accord in the Temple, and while they were singing—notice that there was no preaching—the Shekinah cloud came and filled the house of the Lord, so that those Levites couldn't go on. I see one of them taking out his handkerchief. He breaks down. The power came upon them so that the service couldn't go on. The glory of God filled that Temple. Now, the moment a man opens his heart,

HIS BODY BECOMES A TEMPLE

for God to dwell in. Christ says (John xiv, 16): "I

will give you another Comforter, that He may abide with you forever." It isn't like coming to a religious meeting like this and staying for a few minutes. "He shall abide." "He shall be in you." Let us believe that these bodies are temples of the Holy Ghost to dwell in. If He doesn't dwell in our hearts it is because we won't have Him—because we are living in some dishonorable thing that grieves the Holy Ghost. I take the ground very firmly that there are three classes of Christians in all our churches. I don't think you will find any church without these three classes. Nicodemus came to Jesus by night, and got life. "How do you know?" Why; the next thing he did was to stand up in the Sanhedrim and defend Christ, saying: "Doth our law judge any man before it hear him, and know what he doeth?" And the death of Christ brought him out bold. He got life; but I think he didn't get life in all its abundance. He just barely got life—he didn't get it in all its fullness. If he had got it in all its fullness I will tell you what would have happened. He would have been brought out of that Sanhedrim. He wouldn't have stayed there. But I suppose he reasoned in this way: "I am in a high position—a position of influence. If I should just confess Christ publicly they would put me out of the Sanhedrim. I will use my influence over the members of the Sanhedrim—my standing and influence here in Jerusalem." And do you know, I believe that is the very curse of the Church of God—this compromising. It is the reason so many Christians are dwarfed and haven't got power. They are thinking of worldly honor, worldly power. My dear friends, what we want is to be ready to step down and out. I believe Nicodemus might have been immortalized if he had been willing to step down and out of that Sanhedrim, as Moses got out of Egypt, and as Abraham got out from his own country—if he had said to his associates: "I believe Jesus is the true Messiah, and I will never allow these men to talk against Him." I believe he was a child of God. He had got life. But He didn't have it in its fullness.

A HIGHER TYPE.

In the fourth chapter of John we find a higher type of Christian. There we read about the woman at the well. She got a living spring, bubbling right up there in her soul. She got so much of the living water that she couldn't hold still, but went among her neighbors, saying: "Come, see a man which told me all things that ever I did." And she turned that town upside down. I see a lot of men in the street talking about politics. This women goes up to them and says: "Come down there to the well. There is a man who has told me all things that ever I did." I can imagine one of these men saying, "I think that woman has gone out of her mind." The fact is, she was just coming into her right mind. She had got so much of the water of life that she couldn't hold her peace. Water always rises to its level. We bring water into this building from away up the mountain, and when it gets into the building it just goes into all parts of it. This woman received so much of the living water that it carried her up into the presence of God, and she became a power in the community. She just went back and published it. I am afraid if we had that woman in some of our churches, people would say: "She has a hard reputation—a pretty bad character." I am afraid some one would say to her: "I think you had better keep still for about six months; and if you turn out all right we will take you in." But she didn't wait. She just began to testify; and see the marvelous results. Many believed on her testimony. "Many more believed because of His own Word."

A STILL HIGHER PLANE.

But now, in the seventh chapter of John, thirty-seventh verse, we read: "In the last day, that great day of the feast, Jesus stood and cried, saying, If any man thirst, let him come unto Me, and drink. He that believeth in Me, as the Scripture hath said, out of his belly shall flow rivers of living water. But this spake He of the Spirit, which they that believe on Him should receive." "If any man thirst" —that takes in you and me—"out of his heart shall flow rivers of living water." Better than showers, isn't it? Better even than a spring. There is a spring up here in the mountain that feeds a little brook, and that brook, as it runs over the rocks, makes quite a little noise. But the grand old Connecticut —I never heard it make a noise in my life in this town; it just flows on in its course—flows right on. That little brook sometimes dries up, with all its noise; but the river goes on day and night, Winter and Summer. I believe it is the privilege of every one to have the Spirit of God resting upon him, so that he will be just like that river. There are two ways of digging a well. One is to dig till you come to water, and stop there, though the water won't last long. Another is, to dig down and down and down till you get a never-failing supply. Some of our boys undertook to dig a well lately. When they got down six or eight feet they struck water. A pump was put in and set pumping, pumping; and very soon the well was pumped dry. Then they went on again with their digging till they struck a rock, and the water burst right up. They thought they had got deep enough that time. But when the pump was set to work, it wasn't many days till the well was dry again. We said we musn't stop till we get to where the water couldn't be exhausted. So we went on down and down till we struck clay, and then gravel, and then flinty rock; and at last we got to a lower stratum that yielded a never-failing supply of water. Now, it is the privilege of every child of God

TO HAVE AN ARTESIAN WELL

that can never be pumped dry. I remember that when I was a boy we used to have to pump water for the cattle. Sometimes a man pumped and pumped, and didn't get anything. You have got to have water in a well before you get it out. Lots of men in the pulpit are pumping, pumping, without any effect; but if you have an artesian well, it just flows itself —springing right up—constraining you to speak.

Some English people once emigrated to a strange country intending to settle. They stopped at one place, but the natives told them they had better not—at a certain season of the year everything dried up there. So they went on until they came to a second place, and were intending to settle there, but again they were told that at a certain season of the year everything dried up. On they went again till they got to a place where the mountains pierced the clouds, and they could always have water. I remember the first time I went to California, I stood in a valley and saw a ranch. I noticed that in one section everything was green—everything was all vegetation. But just where you crossed a fence, everything was dried up. It was another ranch, and there was hardly a green thing there. I thought that was very curious, and I said to a farm hand: "Can you explain that?—how on one side of the fence things are all green and on the other side all dried up?" "Oh, yes," said the farm hand; "this man irrigates—he brings water down from the mountain, and just irrigates his farm. That man don't." I think that is the way with a good many Christians in the churches. Some are all dried up; but others have got a secret communication between their souls and Heaven, and God sends the water to them and

KEEPS THEM ALWAYS FRESH.

You may be as dry as Gideon's fleece—all dried up—no power at all; but it is the privilege of each one of us to have the dew of Heaven resting upon us all the while. That is what God wants. Are you thirsty?

I sometimes wish we had in all our churches a meeting for hungry and thirsty Christians. I would put a man at the door so as not to let anybody else in. Let him ask every one: "Are you hungry? Are you thirsty?" They wouldn't know what you meant, some of them. Lots of people go to prayer-meeting because it is customary. They go year after year—go for nothing, and get nothing. They are not in earnest about anything. Now, it seems to me that if we could have a meeting in all our churches of two, three, four, or five Christians, dead in earnest—wanting the baptism of the Spirit, and the power of God resting upon them—there would be a wonderful difference. If they were really in earnest in asking for the gift of the Holy Ghost they would get it. But, I tell you, you have got to stoop to get that. God isn't going to give it to those who are careless and indifferent. But if you and I really want it—want it above everything else—then I believe God will give it. "Blessed are they which do hunger and thirst after righteousness; for they shall be filled." Are you hungry and thirsty after righteousness? I like that "shall be." "They shall be filled." My brother, are you filled? Put the question right to yourself.

"ARE YOU FILLED?"

I think I could have said "Amen" to almost everything in this morning's service; but I couldn't quite agree with Dr. Gordon when he said a man could empty himself. I have heard a great many people say we should empty our hearts so as to let the Holy Spirit come in. Well; I know I can't empty my heart. I can't get pride out of my heart. I can't get jealousy out of my heart. I wish I could. I haven't got the power. But if a man desires above everything else that he may grow smaller and smaller as John the Baptist did—if it his desire that he shall decrease and Christ increase; then I believe the Lord will pour the water down so that it will crowd out all these things. Sometimes in trying to make a pump work I used to see if I could pump all the air out so as to get the water up. After trying a while that way, I would get some water and pour it in from the top, and that would crowd the air out. When a man finds that he can't empty his heart, what he wants is just to let the water in from above. Get under the fountain. Let the living flood come down upon us. It will drive out conceit—drive out everything. Oh, yes; what we want is to get under the fountain. "I will pour floods upon the dry ground." "I will pour water upon him that is thirsty." We can every one of us get a baptism of the Spirit. You remember that when Christ met His disciples after the resurrection, He breathed upon them, saying: "Receive ye the Holy Ghost." Suppose they had said: "We *have* received the Holy Ghost. It was by the power of the Holy Ghost we left all and followed Thee." "Ah," He would have said, "I have yet greater blessings in store for you." I hear people ask, "Have you got the second blessing?" But a second blessing isn't enough. There may be

A GREAT MANY BLESSINGS.

I think a good many people make a mistake in stopping there. Suppose that when Christ breathed upon His disciples, saying, "Receive ye the Holy Ghost," Peter had said, "Lord, we have got it now. You have breathed upon us. Now we are ready to go out and preach. Men will be converted by the power of the Holy Ghost. We are ready to go." "Ah, Peter," He would have said, "I am going to give it to you in greater measure. Tarry at Jerusalem." Suppose Peter had preached before the descent of the Holy Ghost at Pentecost, what do you think would have happened? I believe there wouldn't have been a soul converted. But the disciples testified at Jerusalem till the Spirit came upon them; and then they began to preach, and multitudes were converted. What was the reason? Why, what was the message? A risen Christ—a glorified Christ. They began to proclaim the tidings that "that same Jesus, whom ye have crucified, God hath made both Lord and Christ." Now, a great many times I hear people say—very good men come to me and say: "But, you know, at Pentecost the Holy Ghost came with a rushing, mighty wind, so that the place was shaken. It isn't Scriptural to pray that the Holy Ghost may come in such power as to shake the place again. We musn't look for miraculous power." But I believe

PENTECOST WAS JUST A SPECIMEN.

I believe if as Christians we had faith, this place might be shaken. If we prayed for Pentecostal power, I believe we could get it—we could get Pentecostal showers right here to-day. In the fourth chapter of Acts, Peter and John were cast into prison. Then they were brought before the Sanhedrim. The rulers didn't dare to put them to death, because the whole city was filled with young converts, so they just said to them: "Now, you can preach all you want to, so long as you don't preach in the name of Jesus." Some preachers get along very well without mentioning the name of Jesus. Their sermons are all about philosophy and morality. But Peter and John didn't know anything about those sciences. They were just fishermen, and knew nothing but Calvary. They were only witnesses. The rulers said to them: "You can preach all you want to, if you don't preach any more in the name of Jesus." Well; they had another prayer-meeting, and they prayed for power to go out and preach boldly. "And when they had prayed, the place was shaken where they were assembled together, and they were all filled with the Holy Ghost." That is the way we want to pray. "What! pray for the supernatural?" Yes; we have got to have supernatural power to proclaim the Gospel. In this fourth chapter of Acts it says the place was shaken again, and those men were all filled again. Now, those men had lost their power, or else they had great capacity—I don't know which—but

THEY WERE FILLED AGAIN.

Suppose I had more power four or five years ago than I have to-day, what ought I to do? Why, as soon as I discovered that, I ought to pray to be filled again. Lots of people are like Samson—shorn of their locks. What did Samson do? He let his hair grow out, and got his strength back again. These men that have lost their power—they can get it back again if they will. Ah, thank God; if He used Peter once, He could use him again. My friends, have you lost your power with God? If you have, don't rest day or night till you get it back again. The greatest honor you can ever have is to have the power of God resting upon you. They say it isn't Scriptural to pray that the place may be shaken—to pray for the Holy Ghost as Peter and John did at Jerusalem. My dear friends, I think it is perfectly Scriptural to pray that the Holy Ghost may fall upon us as it fell upon them. Have you worked hard day after day, and seen little results? The power of the Holy Ghost is what you want. Here is a brother from Texas, who tells me he hasn't got power. Oh, dear brother, you can get this power. Here is a brother from South Carolina, who wants to see a great work of God in that State. My brother, you needn't send for this man or that man to go down to South Carolina. You can get this power, and then go out yourself in the name of Jehovah. Here is a lady from Tennessee, who is burdened for that State. My dear sister, pray that the Spirit may fall upon you, and then you can be a mighty instrument for God in that old State. I don't think we have

GOT THE FAINTEST IDEA

what God wants to do with us. We haven't begun to understand the meaning of that passage: "Greater things than these shall ye do." When the Spirit came upon those disciples they were to do greater things than Jesus Christ did. I used to think there could be no greater things than the miracles of Christ; but the longer I live the more it seems to me that the greatest miracle this world has ever seen is that revival at Pentecost. Three thousand Jews converted in one day!—with their minds set against God, their wills set against God, their hearts set against God. They hated with a perfect hatred the name of Jesus. They thought He wasn't fit to walk the streets of Jerusalem. And yet three thousand of those men were converted under one sermon. That was one of the greatest miracles this world has ever seen. I suppose when Christ ascended from this earth He left in the world not more than a thousand disciples. We only read of three hundred. Yet here were three thousand in one day! And that was only the beginning. I was rejoiced to hear Dr. Gordon speak about our getting the first fruits. I don't know what might not happen if this audience should rise as one man and say, "God helping us, we are going into the harvest field. We will buckle on the whole armor, and preach the risen Christ— preach the glorified Christ—tell the people that Christ has been down here in this dark world; that He suffered and died, that He burst asunder the bonds of death, led captivity captive, and now sits on the Throne." Why, do you know, that there are people around here who don't know that—don't know Christ came out of Joseph's sepulchre. Hundreds of people right in this town don't know Christ is out of Joseph's sepulchre. Let us go and preach it. My dear brother,

WOULD YOU LIKE TO GET ANOINTED?

I believe if you pray for this anointing, the Holy Ghost will just come upon you so that every time you speak some one will bless you—every time you open your lips your testimony will have power. Wouldn't you like power? Wouldn't you like to be used of God? Wouldn't you like to see God looking down from his throne, and smiling—just blessing you? If you would, do you know what to do? Let your will be swallowed up in His will. Say to Him: "Lord, use me. I want to be Thine for time and eternity. I want to be Thine soul and body. I want that Thou shouldst take me and fill me." If you ask Him, the Lord will fill you. He wants to do it. You remember, when Elijah was taken away, what happened. Elisha was greatly afflicted to think Elijah was going to leave him. Elijah says to Elisha, "Stay here. I am going to Bethel." Elisha says, "As the Lord lives, I will not leave thee." Elijah says, "Then let's go to Bethel, and see how the prophets are getting along." When they get to Bethel, Elijah says, "Now, you stay here, and I'll go to Jericho." There was a school of young prophets at Jericho, like the school we have here at Mount Hermon. Elisha says, "As the Lord lives I will go with you." The two men go on to Jericho together. At Jericho, the sons of the prophets come to Elisha and say, "Do you know that your master is to be taken away to-day?" "Sh—sh—," says Elisha, "I know all about it." Presently Elijah turns and says, "Elisha, you stay here, and I will go over to the Jordan and worship." Elisha says, "As the Lord lives, and as thy soul lives, I will go with you." So the two go down to the Jordan together. As they walk on, they talk. I have often wished their conversation had been put on record. I like to think about it. I have an idea it was something like this. Elijah says to Elisha: "Is there anything you want? Don't be afraid to ask. You seem to be very timid." Elisha says: "Yes, there is something I want." "Well, don't be afraid to ask.

YOU SHALL HAVE WHATEVER YOU WANT."

My friends, what a statement? "All you ask for. Make a request, and you will have all you ask for." Well, what did he ask? Did he ask for as much of the Spirit as Elijah had? That would have been a great thing. Talk about kings. Kings are in the habit of ordering their subjects around. Here was a subject who was in the habit of ordering kings around. Ah! a man who is in communion with God has power. Talk about the power of Cæsar, Napoleon, Alexander—the great generals and warriors of this earth. Why, it is nothing to the power of the man who is in communion with God. Elijah wasn't going to ask for a small thing. I suppose he thought: "Now, Elijah has given me a blank check; I will fill it out." So he says: "I want a double portion of Thy spirit." I can see Elijah turn around to him in surprise, and say: "You have asked me a hard thing." But he says: "If you see me when I am taken from you, you shall have it." "Then," says Elisha, "you'll not get away without my seeing you." He wanted a double portion of Elijah's spirit, and he was determined to get it. So he took good care to see him in the chariot, and he did see him. Well, they go down to the banks of the river together—arm in arm, like David and Jonathan. Some wonderful stories have taken place on that river; one of the most wonderful is going to take place now. The two prophets march boldly into the water, and go over dry shod. Fifty of the prophets are up there on the side hills. There they sit watching. They see this wonderful miracle. I suppose when they saw Elijah and Elisha go through the bed of that river dry shod, all their talk was about Elijah. They had hardly ever heard of Elisha. He was only an ordinary farmer—just living on Elijah. He hadn't performed any miracle, for any he had ever performed had been associated with Elijah. But as Elijah and Elisha go on together—talking and talking—suddenly there comes a chariot from Heaven, and bears Elijah away. Elisha is not going to let him go away without letting him know he sees him; so he lifts up his voice and cries: "My father, my father! the chariot of Israel and the horsemen thereof." He sends his voice right up after him.

AH! ELIJAH HEARS HIM.

He takes off his mantle, and throws it down to Elisha. Elisha sees the old mantle lying there on the ground. He picks it up and puts it on. I suppose when those fifty prophets see him coming out of the desert alone, they say: "Well, Elijah has been caught up. We'll never see him again, and we'll never see any more like him." When Elisha walks down to the bank of the river, they say: "He never can cross it. The Jordan won't divide for him. There is no bridge for him to walk on—and there's no boatman to take him over. How is he going to get across that stream?" Elisha stands on the bank of the river. I see him lift up his voice to God in prayer, saying: "Lord God of Elijah, hear me! This promised double portion of His spirit has come. Let me test it now." And the power of God upholds him. The Jordan obeys him. He starts into the stream, and goes through it dry shod. As he comes up out of the river the fifty prophets lift up their voices, and they say: "The spirit of Elijah is upon Elisha." But he had more than the spirit of Elijah. Elisha performed just twice the number of miracles that Elijah did.

My friends, the God of Elijah is on the throne. Jesus Christ has come down from Heaven since then; and it is so wonderful to ask for the influence of the Spirit? Why, we ought to have ten times more power than Elijah had. Yes; we ought to have a hundred times more power than Elijah and Elisha had. Let us pray for this double portion of the Spirit. The difficulty is, we have been living on a lower plane. Let us pray that God will fill us with the Holy Ghost. Let us pray that He will send the Spirit into our cold churches and Sabbath-schools, that are now so stiff and formal. Let us pray God that we will have power to overcome this stiffness. Let us pray God that streams of salvation shall break out all over the country. Let us pray to the God of Elijah, and let us pray that the fire may come down and burn up all the dross in our hearts—all that is not pleasing in the sight of God—and that we may be filled with the Holy Spirit. Let us bow our heads.

Dr. Pierson then led in prayer.

Dr. Pentecost followed in a very able and interesting address on the same subject.

ON SANCTIFICATION.

On Wednesday forenoon, Dr. Munhall, of Indianapolis, spoke on "Sanctification," as follows: "Some important truths have fallen into disfavor among Christian people, because of the absurd views of the extremists. When a pendulum swings too far on one side, it will be sure to swing too far on the other. Because of the strange notions of certain Adventurists and faith-healers, the Christian Church has allowed itself to lose sight altogether of the doctrines of healing by faith and the Second Coming. What we want to do is to find out the truth for ourselves, regardless of prejudice. Sanctification is clearly enjoined in Scripture. (See Leviticus xi, 44; I Thess. iv, 3; and I Pet. i, 13–16.) Christians cannot be used without sanctification. (Exodus xxix, 44; John xvi, 19; I Tim. ii, 21.) The words "sanctification," "consecration," and "holiness," in their primary sense, are used interchangeably. As to the primary meaning, there is involved the thought of dedication. (II Sam. viii, 11; Lev. xxvii, 28.) In the secondary meaning, the ideas are embraced of justification, sanctification, etc. Then, considering the question as related to our standing before God, he refered to the following texts: Ex. xxix, 37; I Thess. ix, 13; I John iv, 17; Jude 24; Col. i, 28. All these passages show that man stands before God justified in virtue of Christ's imputed righteousness. In contradistinction from that, a sanctified person stands before God possessing imparted righteousness. See I Tim. ii, 19; Rom. viii, 13; II Cor. ix, 27; Gal. v, 24. These passages all show what is required of us after justification, in the direction of sanctification. Our greatest enemy is the old man. No one should say, "I am sanctified, and therefore cannot sin." A sanctified man is like a field in which the tops of the weeds have been cut off. The roots are there, and under rain and sunshine they will spring up again. Luther was asked if he was not afraid of the Pope. He said he was more afraid of the Pope inside his own heart than of the Pope at Rome. I am more troubled over Munhall than I am over any of my neighbors. In a judicial sense, the old man was put to death in the person of Christ. (Gal. v, 24; Rom. vi, 6.) Rom. vi, 11, indicates how this fact may be made of practical value to us. The old man is not dead, but he is to be reckoned as dead by the exercise of faith. On our unquestioning and continuous faith in this truth depends the real death of the old man in us, if we yield ourselves to the will of God to do what He wishes in us. God, who saves the sinner, can keep him from the domination of sin. It is God who sanctifies. (I Thess. v, 23). Sanctification is in Christ. I Cor. i, 30. It is of the Spirit. (II Thess. ii, 13). It is through the truth (John xvii, 17). It is by faith (Gal. iii, 5).

Now, as to the results. The results of sanctification **are: 1.** Separation (II Cor. vi, 17). 2. Emancipation from love of the world (I John ii, 15). 3. A forgiving spirit (Eph. iv, 32). 4. Purity of speech (Eph. v, 4). 5. Cleanliness of body (II Cor. viii, 1). 6. Weights laid aside (Heb. xii, 1). 7. Life, characterized by good works and zeal for Christ (Heb. xiii, 21). Wearing a sour countenance is not sanctification. Some people are so sanctified they forget to work. When a man is so infatuated with sanctification that he cannot work for Christ, he is simply infatuated with himself. We want zeal. We want "cranks" like John the Baptist. Let us get out of Egypt by a Red Sea deliverance, and into the promised land.

At the close Dr. Munhall called upon those who had either dedicated themselves to God or wished to do so to rise. Nearly all arose.

Dr. Pentecost followed in a few remarks, laying stress upon the fact that our sanctification is in Christ. We are too much given to seeking experiences for their sake alone. What we want is the giver. He told a story of how he used to come home from his evangelistic tours, always bringing his little daughter a present. He noticed, however, with pain, that she seemed to care more for the presents than for himself—rushing to examine his satchel before greeting him. So one time he came home without any present. She asked what he had brought her. Said he: "I have brought you myself." She comprehended his meaning, and burst into tears—never having realized how the habit was growing upon her. Let us seek Christ—be identified with Christ, and sanctification will follow.

Mr. Moody said: "I'd like to give you my short-cut to sanctification in five words, 'Be filled with the Spirit.'"

At the afternoon meeting brief addresses were made by various Christian workers. Mr. Albert Woodruff, of Brooklyn, spoke of Sunday-school work in Europe. Mr. F. G. Ensign, of Chicago, told of the work of the American Sunday-school Union in the Northwest. Professor Wayland, of Yale College, New Haven, spoke strongly on the utility of mission Sunday-schools in the neglected parts of large cities, in connection with parent churches.

DR. PIERSON ON PRAYER MEETINGS.

The question, "How to Conduct Prayer Meetings?" was discussed, Dr. Pierson making the first address. He said that in Bethany Church, Philadelphia, they had a prayer-meeting attended by six to eight hundred people, and he regarded the prayer-meeting as next in importance to the proclaiming of the Gospel. First, he said, drop all stiffness and formality. Let the leader avoid sermonizing or lecturing. He should just open the meeting with a brief exposition of some passage of Scripture. Let him cultivate a colloquial style of speaking. The leader should come to the meeting fresh from his closet. Let him carry the atmosphere of Heaven to the meeting with him. It would be well if the people would come from their closets, too. Then there would be none of the Spirit of criticism. Have good, cheerful, lively singing. Then bring out testimony from young Christians. Let them bring reports from any special work in which they are engaged. That will give you a subject for prayer. People sometimes go to prayer-meeting with the vaguest possible notion of what to pray for. Let your young people tell how they are getting along in their special work for Christ. That will incite prayer by furnishing objects of supplication. Let the prayers be short and right to the point. We have too many formal, systematic and stereotyped prayers. What we want is to get people to leave off the "preamble and resolutions." Let them begin right in the middle, and stop without thinking how they are going to close. In that way you can have fifteen or twenty people pray in the course of five or ten minutes. Let each one pray for the one burden on his heart. Don't let any one pray too long. It is hard sometimes to get people to rise to their feet; it is often a great deal harder to get them to sit down. If a man doesn't know how time goes, get some one to pull his coat tail. It does no harm to stop in the middle of a sentence. Sometimes it helps immensely.

REMARKS BY MR. MOODY.

Mr. Moody said: There is another thing we want, and that is ventilation. A good many prayer-meetings are failures. There is a deadness in them. What is the reason? Bad air. Many prayer-meetings are held in the basements of churches where there is bad air—you would think it was the same air year after year. People can't help going to sleep. Now, I think the minister ought to take an interest in getting fresh air. He ought to see that the audience don't lack for ventilation, and that the air is sweet. When a man has been working hard out in the fields all day, in a pure atmosphere, and then comes into a room where the air is close, the chances are that he will go to sleep before the meeting is one-quarter over. Another thing: Have new hymns. Don't sing only "Rock of Ages," and "Jesus, Lover of My Soul." I don't see how people can go on singing the same hymns year in and year out. In a great many prayer-meetings they have about twelve hymns that they sing year after year. We want variety. Get new hymns and solos as well as the old ones. Another thing: Let the leader give the meeting a sort of key-note, and then get out of the way. Many men kill a meeting by talking too much. They tell you they are unprepared, and you will find it out before they get through. They have no business to be unprepared. Don't talk, talk, just to fill up the time. Time is precious. Another thing: If you have a man who is in the habit of making a long prayer, go right to him and tell him you can't have it. More meetings are made cold by long prayers than by any other one thing. My experience is, a man who makes a prayer fifteen minutes long in public doesn't pray much at home. A man in the habit of praying at home knows how to pray short. He won't take much time to make his wants known. Now, you know very well that young people don't come into the churches as they ought to. What keeps them out? Long prayers. If a man makes long prayers, tell him you can't allow it. You don't want to hurt his feelings? Better hurt his feelings than hurt the cause of Christ. If a man can't take a rebuke, he isn't in the right spirit of prayer. A man once said to me: "I am carried away by the Spirit, and I forget myself." "Well," I said, "I will have a man sit next to you and pull your coat." We arranged it that way; and the next time, a man pulled his coat several times, so that he only prayed two or three minutes. When a man has prayed five minutes, the bulk of the people will pray to have him stop. They can't think of what he is praying about—they are thinking "I wish that man would stop," and, by the time he stops, their minds have got into another channel. It seems to me a man ought not to pray longer than a minute. A minute is one hundred and eighty words. Another thing: If a man doesn't stand well in the community, don't let him take part. Go right to him and say: "You must clear up your record before you take part." A good many churches have lost all their power because they don't look after this. If a man doesn't pay his debts, if he isn't honest in his business transactions, upright in his moral character, you don't want him to take part. These men drive people from the prayer-meeting. Now we want to talk about music.

After a hymn, Mr. Moody introduced the subject of music. Addresses were made by Mr. H. L Hastings, of Boston; Mr. McGranahan, and Mr. Sankey. Mr. Sankey also answered a number of questions put to him by several of the leading speakers and by persons in the audience.

The Rev. Jacob Freshman, of New York, described his work among the eighty thousand Jews of the metropolis. Mr. Moody became greatly interested in his recital, and called for contributions in aid of his work. Mr. Freshman received $171, and afterwards the gift of an organ from Colonel Estey, of Brattleboro, Vt.

THE SECOND COMING.

Mr. Moody, in opening the forenoon meeting, said he hoped all would listen in a kindly spirit. If the post-millenarians—those who believe Christ will not come till the end of the thousand years—had anything to say, they would have a chance. He had held the pre-millennial theory since 1867.

The Rev. W. W. Clark, of Staten Island, exhibited two colored charts which brought out vividly the marvelous correspondence between prophecy and history in relation to the second coming of Christ. The belief in the pre-millennial coming of Christ, he said, is the corner-stone of all interpretation of prophecy. The dispensations displayed in the charts were: That of conscience—from Adam to Abraham; that of promise—from Abraham to Moses; that of law—from Moses to Christ; that of the Church—from the day of Pentecost to the second coming; that of tribulation—from Christ's coming for His saints to His appearing with them; that of the Millennium—covering the one thousand years when Christ shall reign on earth, at the ending of which the wicked dead shall be raised and judged before the great white throne. Jesus told His disciples to look for His coming. That duty is incumbent upon us to-day. The translation of Enoch and Elijah was probably designed to show us how the translation of the righteous who may be living when Christ comes shall occur.

Dr. Pierson said he opposed this doctrine stoutly for twenty years, but now he believed he was then in error. He was not bound to any system of details, however. He simply believed Christ is coming a second time, at the end of the present dispensation. His belief in this doctrine had so strengthened his ardor in behalf of foreign missions that he was sometimes thought fanatical on that subject. From this doctrine we get a conception of the work that is to be done in this dispensation. Let us get hold of the idea that the Church is to be taken out of the world. The Church is becoming worldly. Don't expect that the world is to be incorporated in Christ; men are to withdraw from the world to reach Christ. Our Lord is to take a people unto Himself out of the world. He believed the greatest inspiration to all kinds of Gospel work lies in this doctrine of the second coming.

Mr. Needham said, in his opinion, when any Christian read the Scriptures for himself, free from prejudice or pre-conceived notions, he was naturally led to a belief in the second coming. Nothing does so much as this doctrine to wean believers from worldly entanglements. If we really believe Christ might come at any moment, we wouldn't be found at theatres and card parties.

In the afternoon Dr. Gordon was the leading speaker. He said he came to believe in this doctrine five years after coming out of a theological seminary, and now considered it as well-grounded as the doctrine of the vicarious atonement. He went into the subject exhaustively, quoting very freely from Scripture. What was the practical bearing of the doctrine? We are told to watch. Sobriety is enjoined. Purity is advised—entreated. The world is being prepared for Christ's coming. Missionaries are kindling flames in China, Japan, Turkey, Africa —all over the globe. He would close in the words of Christ Himself: "What I say unto one, I say unto all, Watch!"

Address to Young Men.*

You will find my text this evening in the sixth chapter of Galatians, seventh, eighth, and ninth verses: "Be not deceived; God is not mocked; for whatsoever a man soweth, that shall he also reap. For he that soweth to his flesh shall of the flesh reap corruption, but he that soweth to the Spirit shall of the Spirit reap life everlasting. And let us not be weary in well doing, for in due season we shall reap, if we faint not." You who were here last Wednesday night remember that we had for our text, "Their rock is not as our rock, even our enemies themselves being judges," and then we tried to find a text which everyone would admit was true. I think that we have one to-night that no infidel, no skeptic, or deist can attack. There are some passages which we do not have to prove by the Word of God, but merely by our own experience. Your own lives will prove many passages in Scripture. You can take up the daily papers and see them fulfilled under your own eyes. This is one of them. Perhaps there has not been a text of Scripture run out in this Tabernacle as this one has. Night after night we have said something about it; night after night

---

* From "Great Joy," by permission of E. B. Treat, Publisher.

Mr. Sankey has sung out, "Whatsoever a man soweth that shall he also reap." My friends, we cannot quote it too often. We want to quote it, and preach it till it gets down to the hearts of the people. Now, it is very natural to be deceived. I suppose there is not a man or woman here but who has been deceived by his or her most intimate friends. You have been deceived by your own friends, and you have been deceived by your enemies, and how many could rise up here and say they have not been deceived by themselves? How many of us have found our own heart more treacherous than anything else? How many of us have not found the truth of that passage, "The heart of man is deceitful above all things, and desperately wicked." We can be deceitful to each other, to our friends and to ourselves, but bear in mind we cannot deceive God. How often does man find that Satan had deceived him? But has he ever found God deceiving him? I have never found a man who has said that he has been or that he has heard of anybody whom God has deceived. How many times has man said he has been deceived by his fellows—by his own treacherous heart; and our experience in this direction only shows that we cannot rely upon man, upon ourselves, but only upon God.

Now, it is a law of nature that if a man sows he will reap what he sows. If a man sows watermelons, he don't look for cauliflowers; if a man sows potatoes, he don't look for cabbages; if he sows onions, he don't look for corn. If he plants potatoes, he expects potatoes; if he sows corn, he looks for corn; or wheat, he expects to reap wheat. So, in the natural world, a man expects to reap what he sows. If a man learns a carpenter's or a builder's trade, he expects to put up buildings for a living. If a man toils and studies hard for a profession—if he is a lawyer, he expects to practice law. He don't expect to have to preach the Gospel for a living. He has been sowing for years, and he expects to reap. As a man sows, so he expects to reap. This the law in the natural world, and so it is with the spiritual: "Blessed are they that mourn, for they shall be comforted;" "Blessed are the peacemakers, for they shall be called the children of God;" "Blessed are they which hunger and thirst for righteousness' sake." Why? Because they shall get rich? No—"for they shall be filled." Now, you will see that a certain result is the product of certain conditions. This is the law which you will find carried out all through the world, in natural and spiritual things. If a man is a thief, you expect to see him come to an ignominious end. If a man is drunken and dissipated, we look, as a natural consequence of his dissipation, to see him go to ruin. Yet men themselves don't see this; their eyes are closed to their folly. A friend who was coming down with me to-night said: "When I look back, I see that I started wrong when I came here. It seems as if I must have been blind. I did not see this till within the last two or three weeks." My friends, that's what Satan does with a man—he just blinds him, and when he has got a man blinded he does anything he wants with him. It is very hard to make men understand this simple truth, that they will have to reap what they sow, especially young men from seventeen to twenty-one. That, you know, is the ugly age. There is more trouble with them then than at any other stage. I remember when I was at that age. I knew a good deal more than my mother or any of my friends. You take a young man at that age, and you'll find he knows a great deal more than his father, his grandfather, or even his great-grandfather, all put together. "He is wise in his own conceit." It is during that ugly age that characters are forming for good or evil; and bear in mind, you young men, that "Whatsoever a man soweth that shall he also reap." If a man sows tares, he has got to reap them. It may not be to-morrow, or next week, or next year, but the time of reaping will assuredly come, and when the reaping time comes you will moan bitterly; then you will like to change places with those Christians whom you despise now. When the reaping time comes you would give a good deal if you could exchange places with the humblest-looking Christian. I suppose that Cain would give a good deal to exchange places with Abel to-night. Do you think Pilate would not like to change places with Elijah, with Obadiah, or Peter, to-night? Don't you think the Emperor Nero would like to exchange places now with Paul? Paul is reaping what he sowed, and so is Nero. All through Scripture you can see proof of this text. Don't you think that the rich man at whose door the beggar Lazarus lay would like to exchange places with that poor Christian now? Bear in mind that you may look upon Christians with contempt, but the time is coming when you will give anything to exchange places with the meanest Christian that walks the streets of Chicago.

I used to believe twenty years ago in this text, but I believe it more now than ever I did. The longer I live the more I become convinced of its awful truth. You know I used to live in Chicago, and I used to go from house to house among the poor, and in going among the poor I gained no little experience of the rich people. In visiting the poor I became acquainted with a good many rich families, and there is scarcely a week passes now but I hear of rich families who have gone down to ruin. Just this afternoon I heard of a family who, twenty years ago, occupied a position among the best. They had a beautiful daughter, who could have adorned any station, and a lovely home, and I heard to-day that they had gone down to ruin. They looked upon Christianity with scorn and contempt. The father brought the children up to treat all religion with contempt, and his sons have gone down to their graves drunkards, and his daughter has died of a broken heart. Yes, a man who sows tares must reap them, and sometimes the harvest is a whirlwind.

Now, just let us divide that text up—not that I want to preach under different heads, but just for the sake of greater clearness. When a man sows he expects to reap. This truth must be admitted first. A farmer that planted grain and never reaped his fields, you would say had gone clear mad. No man sows that doesn't expect to reap. That is just what he does expect to do. The next point: A man always expects to reap more than he sowed. If he sows a handful of grain, he expects to get from that handful a bushel, and if he sows a bushel he expects a harvest of five hundred bushels. And just so it is in spiritual matters. If a man scatters handfuls of tares in spiritual things, his spiritual harvest will be bushels of tares, and not wheat. Whatever he sows he shall reap; just that and nothing more; and if he sows the wind he must reap the whirlwind. A man must expect a harvest of just the kind that his seed is; and this great law is even more true of spiritual growth than of natural growth. If a man is bad and corrupt in his thoughts, you can tell precisely what his deeds will be.

If a man is profane and blasphemous, look to his children to be the same; if a father is a lying man, his children will grow up to deceive him just as he deceived others. A bad boy is too often the living penalty of the sins of his parents; they have sown and watered, and now he is reaping the punishment. Another point: if a man sows, he must reap the fruit, no matter how ignorant he may claim to be, or really be, of the nature of the seed. A plea of ignorance won't do. You sow tares and think it wheat, but nothing but tares will spring up. You may call it wheat, or rye, or grain, of whatever name you please, but you get nothing but weeds and tares. You must look to what kind of seed you are sowing, for neither ignorance nor any other excuse can make tares bring forth wheat. And now, see how true that is, in regard not only to individuals but nations. Nations are only collections of individuals, and what is true of the part in regard to character is always true of the whole. In this country our forefathers planted slavery in the face of an open Bible, and didn't we have to reap? When the harvest came nearly half a million of your young men were buried, many of them in a nameless grave. Didn't God make this nation weep in the hour of gathering the harvest, when we had to give up our young men, both North and South, to death; and every household almost had an empty chair, and blood, blood, blood, flowed like water for four long years? Ah, our nation sowed, and how in tears and groans she had to reap!

Then look at that king in Egypt. He made a decree that all the male infants should be put to death; and to death they were put, with all the horrors that hatred and jealousy could invent. It was terrible. Well, now, I suppose some people think it strange that God didn't punish Egypt with swift destruction. But look, the punishment only tarried. The mill of God grinds slow, but it grinds exceedingly small; in eighty years cast your eye on that miserable land. God's vengeance at length came down, and ruin along with it. In every house in Egypt the first born was slain, from the palace to the lowest hovel. There still lived a God, and this immutable law of His had still to be executed; they had to reap just what they had sown. Then, sometimes the mill is not so slow. Sometimes the punishment comes rapidly—like lightning. No sooner did the voice ascend that Cain had killed his brother, than God came down and put a mark upon his forehead. Scarcely had Judas betrayed his master than he came back with his thirty pieces of silver, and, torn with remorse, threw them down before the priests, and went out and hung himself. You will find that very often judgment and destruction come very sudden—come like a flash from the throne of God. I remember, in the north of England, a prominent citizen told me a sad case that happened there in the town of Newcastle-on-Tyne. It was about a young boy. He was very young, but he said he was too young to go to a Sunday-school. He was an only child. The father and mother thought everything of him, and did all they could for him. But he fell into bad ways; he took up with evil characters, and finally got to running with thieves. He didn't let his parents know about it. One night they got him to break into a saloon—what the people there call a public house. They stood outside while he entered the house and broke into the till. He was caught, and in one short week he was tried, convicted, and sent for ten years to Van Dieman's Land. His term of servitude expired, and he returned to his native land. He came to the town where his mother and father used to live, and soon stood at the door of his old home. He had been gone ten years, and what a change he found there. My friends, ten years seem a short time, but look back over the period of ten years in your lives, and see how many changes have taken place. He went to his old home and knocked, but a stranger came to the door and stared him in the face. "No, there's no such person lives here, and where your parents are I don't know," was the only welcome he received. Then he turned through the gate, and went down the street, asking even the children that he met about his folks, where they were living, and if they were well. But everybody looked blank. Ten years had rolled by, and though that seemed perhaps a short time, how many changes had taken place! There where he was born and brought up, he was now an alien, and unknown even in his old haunts. But at last he found a couple of townsmen that remembered his father and mother, and they told him the old house had been deserted long years ago; that he had been gone but a few months before his father was confined to his house, and very soon after died broken-hearted; and that his mother had gone out of her mind. He went to the mad-house where his mother was, and went up to her and said: "Mother, mother, don't you know me? I am your son!" But she raved, and slapped him on the face, and shrieked, "You are not my boy!" and then raved again and tore her hair. He left the asylum more dead than alive, so completely broken-hearted that he died in a few months. Yes, the fruit was long growing, but at last it ripened to the harvest like a whirlwind, and vengeance made quick work of it. The death harvest was reaped.

But bear in mind what I have said to-night, and be not doubters, even if the harvest is slow. Let me read you the passage: "Because sentence against their evil deeds is not executed speedily, therefore the hearts of the sons of men are fully set in to do them evil. Though a sinner do evil a hundred times and his days be prolonged, yet surely I know that it shall be well with them that fear God, which fear before Him, but it shall not be well with the wicked, neither shall He prolong His days, which are a shadow, because he feareth not before God."

My friends, if you sow in the flesh you will reap disappointment; you will reap gloom, despair and remorse; the harvest will be death and hell—that will be the end; but if you sow of the Spirit, you will reap peace, joy, happiness, life everlasting; for God has said it. There are a great many things in this world that we are not sure of—we are sure of nothing, I may say. I am not sure that I will finish this sermon; I am not sure that I may go home to-night; we cannot say, positively, that the sun will rise to-morrow morning. Yes, my friends, there are a great many things that we are not sure of; but there is one thing we are sure of, for God has said it. You can be sure that your sins will find you out. If we don't judge ourselves and confess our sins they will find us out. "He that covereth his sins shall not prosper;" that is God's decree.

Now I have been censured by many for advising two men who had committed crime to go back and confess their sin. One man the other day was cursing me for doing so. "A pretty kind of religion this is," he said; but my friends, if a man has gone into a court and publicly perjured himself, he cannot serve God till he publicly confesses it. If he has sinned in public he must confess his sin in public. These men have gone back and written letters full of encouragement. One of them says, "Perhaps I will go to the penitentiary for three years, but what is that in comparison to the burden I would have carried had I not confessed." Now bear in mind that if you cover your sin you shall not prosper; you may keep it secret but it will eventually come out. Look at the sons of Jacob! Look at them when they took away their brother, and after they had delivered him into slavery, see them coming back. How much they must have suffered with their secret during those twenty years. What misery they must have endured as they looked during all these years at their old father sorrowing for his son Joseph. They knew the boy had not been killed—they knew he was in slavery. For twenty years the sin was covered up, but at last it came back upon them. God had in the meantime been doing everything for Joseph; he had raised him nearly to the throne of Egypt. A famine struck the land of the father, and the old man sent his sons down to Egypt to get corn. God was at work. He was making these men bring their their own sin home to themselves. Their conscience smote them and they confessed in the presence of Joseph that their sin had found them out. Twenty years after it was committed that sin was resurrected, and with it they were brought face to face. My friends, be sure at once that your sin will find you out. God has said it, and if He says a thing He means it. "He that covereth his sins shall not prosper," I can imagine some one saying to Absalom when he started out to fight his father, "you shouldn't do this; you are committing a sin, and it will find you out." I can see that young friend looking down upon that man with scorn and contempt. The idea of his sins ever finding him out, ever coming back upon him. He probably would have said, "That man's talking for effect," like a good many say of me. You will hear some people say, "Well, now, any man who knows anything about education knows well enough that Moody is only preaching for effect." If a man tells me I am preaching for effect, I say, "Amen, Amen." That's what I am trying to do; what does a man preach for if it is not for effect. I am trying to create an effect and so wake you up to your condition, and if you don't wake up, the reaping time will come upon you, the whirlwind of troubles and sorrows will rush over your defenseless head, and then you will reap what you have sown in years gone by.

But let me say that if you are willing to confess your sins—I don't care what the sin may be—God is willing and ready to take it away. As I have said, there has been a great deal of talk about my interfering with those prisoners lately. Some one has said in speaking about that man in Ohio, "Well, that is a queer kind of Christianity, to send a man away back to the penitentiary to suffer?" Let me say here that that young man has said in his last letter: "I think I am happier than you are, Mr. Moody; God is helping me to bear the burden; God is answering my prayers." My friends, it was a great deal better for that man to confess his crime than to try to hide it away. If a man commits a crime he should suffer the penalty. I must suffer the penalty if I break my arm in fighting. The man with whom I fought may forgive me for fighting with him, but I have to suffer all the same with my arm. A man got into a quarrel and got crippled, and some time ago he became converted, but although God has forgiven him his sin he has to remain a cripple all his life. So a man must reap what he sows. I heard of an illustration that just helps me out here. Suppose I have a field, and I say to a man, "I want you to sow that field with wheat." The man has become very angry—all out of sorts with me, and when he sows that wheat he puts in a lot of tares. When the wheat has come up I see among it a great many tares. I say to him, "Did you sow these tares?" "Well," he says, "I will confess; yes, sir, I did it; I sowed these tares; I will confess it instead of covering it up; but, sir, I am very sorry;" and I forgive him. But when the wheat has to be harvested I make the man reap the tares also.

You know how David fell. No man rose so high and fell so far, I think. God took him from the sheepfold and put him upon a throne. He took him from obscurity and made him King of Israel and Judea; gave him lands in abundance, and would have given him more if he had wanted them. He was on the pinnacle of glory, and honored among men. But one day, while looking out of a window, he saw a woman with whom he became enamored.

He yielded to the temptation, and ordered her to be brought into the palace, and committed the terrible sin of adultery. After that, as is the case with all men who commit a sin, he had to commit another to cover it up, so he laid plans to kill her husband, and ordered him to be put in a position in the ranks of his army so that he could be killed. Months rolled away, and one day Nathan came into the palace of the king. I can imagine that David was glad to see him. Nathan began to tell him about two men who dwelt in a certain city. The one was rich, the other poor; one had herds and flocks, and the other had only a little ewe lamb, and he went on to tell how this rich man seized this ewe lamb, all that the poor man had, and slew it. I can see the anger of David as it flashed from his eye when he heard the story, and he cried: "As the Lord liveth, the man that hath done this thing shall surely die." He turned to Nathan, and in tones of thunder demanded who the man was. "Thou art the man," was the reply of Nathan. David had convicted himself. "The man who did this thing shall die." Then the Lord said: "I will raise up evil against thee out of thine own house, because thou hast kept this thing secret." Soon after, the hand of death was put upon that house; not only did death enter his house; but it wasn't long before his eldest son committed adultery with his sister, and another committed murder—murdered his own brothers, and went off into a foreign land into exile. Then he got up a rebellion and drove the king from the throne, and at last died and was buried like a dog, and they heaped stones upon his resting place. "Whatsoever a man soweth, that shall he also reap." David committed adultery, so did his son; David committed murder, his son did the same. He was paid back in his own coin. He learned the truth of this passage: "Whatsoever a man soweth, that shall he also reap." Why, I hear things every day in this city of Chicago that make my ears tingle. I heard of three cases within the last six hours where men who have gone to the altar and sworn before God to love, cherish, and protect the women who became their wives—who have become, some of them, mothers of children—and, because these men have seen other women they like better, they have cast off these women whom they have sworn before God to love. Do you think there is a God in heaven? Do you think that God is not going to punish these men? They may go on in their career—punishment may not come for a little while, but the wheels of judgment are going on, and retribution will come. Some of these heart-broken wives say it is hard. Wait a little while. His eyes cover all the earth, and man cannot deceive Him. He has said: "Whatsoever a man soweth, that shall he also reap." High heaven has decreed it, and I beg of you, if you have committed this sin, go and cry to the God of mercy. Go, confess it; don't try to cover it up. Let every sin be brought out; if you don't, your own conscience will turn against you by and by.

When I was in London I went into a wax-work there—Mme. Tussaud's—and I went into the chamber of horrors. There were wax figures of all kinds of murderers in that room. There was Booth, who killed Lincoln, and many of that class; but there was one figure that I got interested in, who killed his wife because he loved another woman, and the law didn't find him out. He married this woman and had a family of seven children, and twenty years passed away. Then his conscience began to trouble him. He had no rest; he could hear his murdered wife pleading continually for her life. His friends began to think he was going out of his mind; he became haggard, and his conscience haunted him, till at last he went to the officers of the law and told them that he was guilty of murder. He wanted to die, life was so much of an agony to him. His conscience turned against him. My friends, if you have done wrong, may your conscience be woke up, and may you testify against yourself. It is a great deal better to judge our own acts and confess them, than go through the world with a curse upon you. And if you to-night will judge your own sin and confess it, He is faithful to forgive. He will forgive every sinner here if you but come to Him in faith, and will blot out all your iniquities.

I was telling of a young man who spoke up in the association one night. He got up at the close of the meeting and said, "Mr. Moody, may I say a few words?" Well, I thought I wouldn't, but then I thought perhaps he has a message from God, and I told him to speak. He went on and urged these young men to accept salvation. "If you have friends praying for you, if you have mothers praying for you, treat them kindly, for you will not always have them with you." Then he went on to tell how he had once a father and mother who loved him dearly, and who prayed continually for him. He was an only child. His father died, and after the burial his mother became more anxious than ever for his salvation. Sometimes she would come to him and put her arms around his neck and say with kindness, "Oh, my boy, I would be so happy if you would only be a Christian, and could pray with me." He would push her away: "No, mother; I'm not going to become a Christian yet; I am going to wait a little longer and see the world." He would try to banish the subject from his mind altogether. Sometimes he would wake up at the midnight hour, and would hear the voice of that mother raised in supplication for her boy: "Oh, God, save my boy; have mercy upon him." At last, this is the way he put it: "It got too hot for him." He saw he had either to become a Christian or run away. And away he ran; and became a prodigal and a wanderer. He heard from her indirectly; he could not let his mother know where he was, because he knew she would have gone to the end of the world to find him. One day he got word that his mother was very sick. He began to think: "Suppose mother should die, I would never forgive myself," and he said, "I will go home," but then he thought, "Well, if I go home, she will be praying at me again, and I can't stay under her roof and listen to her prayers," and his proud, stubborn heart would not let him go. Months went on, and again he heard indirectly that his mother was very sick. His conscience began to trouble him. He knew he would never forgive himself if he didn't go home, and he finally determined. There were no railroads, and he had to go in a stage-coach. At night he got into the town. The moon was shining, and he could see the little village before him. The mother's home was about a mile from where he landed, and on his way he had to pass the village grocery, and as he went along, he thought he would pass through the grave-yard and see his father's grave. "What," he thought, "if my mother has been laid there." When he got up to the grave he saw by the light of the moon a new-made grave. He felt the turf, and the earth was fresh and soft. He knew who had been laid there, and for once in his life the thought flashed upon him, "Who will pray now for my lost soul; my mother and father lie there, and they are the only ones who ever prayed for me." "Young man," said he, "I spent that night at my mother's grave, and before the sun rose, my mother's God had become my God. But I can never forgive myself for murdering my mother, although Christ has forgiven me." My friends, that poor fellow had to reap what he had sowed.

I may be speaking to-night to some young men whose mother perhaps just now is in her closet, wrestling in prayer for you. Bless God, boy, for that mother. Do not treat that mother contemptuously; do not deny her prayer to-night; do not make light of your mother's cries to God this night. God's best gift on earth to you is that praying mother. She is your dearest, most unselfish friend in all the world. Will you not heed her pleading prayer? Come out like a man; come to your mother's Saviour, and take Him to be your God. May the God of heaven convict you of sin, and draw you to Himself, and this will be the best night you've had upon earth.

How many are there in this room to-night who have moral courage to stand up right in this Tabernacle and say, "Pray for me?" How many in this room to-night would like to become Christians? How many are there in this room now who would like to have prayer for them, beseeching prayer, that God will save them? I am going to lead in prayer, and as many as would like to have prayer —personal prayer, to God, will just rise. You can just stand right up one after another. Never mind if there is but one of you; just remain standing. There's another who's got moral courage to rise tonight. Just stand up, will you, and remain so while others join you. There, there, friends, don't get up as if you were ashamed or scared; rise up and show me and God that you are in earnest. I would like to see every man out of Christ rising right up here. There's another in the gallery, and another; well, keep rising; I would sit here all night and see you rise up in the galleries there and everywhere. Every man and woman in this assembly, every boy, who would like to be a Christian, will you just rise now, all of you.

How to be Saved.[*]

I wonder how many of these people here this afternoon would like to be saved? I am not going to ask those who would rise. I do not know whether anyone would have courage enough to rise, and by that act say, "I would like to be saved." Perhaps you say to yourselves, "If that man will just tell me the way how I can be saved this afternoon, I will be saved." I believe one reason why so few are saved, is because they do not come out to the meetngs expecting to be saved. They do not come for that purpose. There was a lady came to our meeting in Philadelphia—to the noon meeting at eleven o'clock; she came early so as to get a good seat. After the meeting was over we had another meeting for women, and she stayed at that. In the afternoon we had another meeting and she stayed at that. She had made up her mind not to leave the meetings until she had found Christ. She did not find Him at that meeting, but she might have found Him. He was offered freely to every one, at all of them. So she stayed at the afternoon meeting, and still no light came. She stayed at the evening meeting and went into the inquiry meeting after-

---

[*] From "Glad Tidings," by permission of E. B. Treat, Publisher.

wards. Between eleven and twelve o'clock she took me by the hand and said, "I will trust Him." And she rejoiced in the Saviour's love. I met her afterwards. There was not a face shown more than hers did. There was a woman who came determined to find Him. When we search for God with all our hearts we are sure to find Him.

I am not going to preach so much of a sermon to-day, as I am going to try to tell you the Way of Life. I had a long talk with a man yesterday who, I really believe, was honestly seeking the Kingdom of God; but the trouble was, he was determined to try to seek Him in his own way, and trying to work the thing out himself, instead of just trusting to Jesus for it. I hope he is here to-night, and that the Lord may bless this little talk to his soul, and that he may to-night sleep safely in the arms of Jesus Christ. It is supremely important to every soul here this day to trust in Christ and be saved. I am going to take up a few Scriptural illustrations. The first is the ark. When I was in Manchester, in one of the inquiry meetings, I went up into the gallery to talk with a few men who were standing together, and who were inquirers of the Way of Life. And while they were standing in a little group around me, there came up another man and got on the outside of the audience, and I thought by the expression of his face that he was skeptical. I did not think he had come to find Christ. But as I went on talking, I noticed the tears trickling down his cheeks. I said, "My friend, are you anxious about your soul's salvation?" He said, "Yes, very." I asked him what was the trouble, and I kept on talking to that one man, thinking that if he could understand me perhaps the others would. He said he wanted to feel all right about it. I explained to him by means of an illustration, and asked him, "Do you see it?" He said "No." I used another, and asked him, "Do you see it yet!" and he said "No" again. I gave still another, and still he said he did not see. I then said, "Was it Noah's feeling that saved him; or was it his ark! Was what saved Noah his righteousness? Was it his life, was it his prayers, was it his tears, was it his feelings, or was it the ark?" He came immediately and grasped me by the hand, and said, "I see it now; it is all right now; I've got to go away on the next train, and I'm in a hurry, but you have made it plain to me; good-bye." And he went off I thought it was so sudden that he could not have understood it. But the next Sunday afternoon he came and tapped me on the shoulder and smiled, and asked me if I remembered him. I said no, that I remembered his face, but could not tell who he was or where I had seen him before. He said, "Do you remember a man that came up into the inquiry-room the other day, and you explained to him how it was Noah's ark that saved him? I did not see any illustration until you used that one, and then I saw it all." I asked him how he was, and he said he had been all right ever since, and that the ark had saved him. I afterwards learned that he was one of the best business men of Manchester. His feelings did not save him. The ark saved him.

I want to prove to you that salvation is instantaneous. It is just as sudden as a man walking through a doorway. One minute he is on this side, the next he is on that side. There was one minute when Noah was exposed to the wrath that was to come over the whole world; but when he went through the doorway of the ark, that moment he was safe. There are many who are trying to make an ark for themselves out of their feelings, out of their own good deeds. But God has provided an ark. If Noah had had to build himself an ark when the flood came, he would have been lost like the rest. A good many of those men who perished when that flood came tried to make arks for themselves, but they all perished helplessly. They tried to make boats and rafts, and tried every way they could to save themselves, but they perished because they were not in the ark that God had appointed. So, to-day, every man and every woman must perish that is not in the ark which God has appointed for their salvation. A knowledge about the ark is not going to help you. A great many persons flatter themselves they are going to be saved because they know a great deal about Jesus Christ. But your knowledge of Him will not save you. Noah's carpenters probably knew as much about the ark as Noah did, and perhaps more. They knew that the ark was strong. They knew it was built to stand the Deluge. They knew it was made to float upon the waters. They had helped to build it. But they were just as helpless when the flood came as men who lived thousands of miles away. Men who lived right in sight of the ark, that knew all about it, perished like the rest, because they were not in the ark. I know something about the different lines of steamers, and I have crossed the Atlantic. Here is another man that has never heard there was such a line of steamers. We both want to go to Europe. My knowledge of a line of steamers does not help me a bit if I do not take the means to go there. You may hear about Christ, but if you do not believe in Christ you cannot be saved. Your knowledge is not going to help you to your salvation. What you want to do is just to make Christ your ark, and then to step into that ark and be saved.

I can imagine you saying, "I do not see how a person can be saved all at once." So, many persons think they have to work themselves out gradually, that they have to do a little here, a little there, and after they have toiled and worked, and have considered the matter prayerfully for some time, they will be more acceptable. The Israelites were told to sprinkle blood upon the door-posts, that the angel might not enter the houses where the blood was to be seen. There was one moment when they had not sprinkled the blood on their door-posts, and when they were exposed to the blight of the destroying angel; and there was another moment when the blood had been sprinkled there, and they were safe. There is a legend told about this which illustrates it very well. It is about a little girl who was the first-born, and consequently who would have been a victim on that night if the protecting blood were not sprinkled on the door-posts of her father's house. The order was that the first-born was to be struck by death all through Egypt. This little girl was sick, and she knew that death would take her, and she might be a victim of the order. She asked her father if the blood was sprinkled on the door-posts. He said it was, that he had ordered it to be done. She asked him if he had seen it there. He said no, but he had no doubt that it was done. He had seen the lamb killed, and had told a servant to attend to it. But she was not satisfied, and asked her father to go and see, and urged him to take her in his arms and carry her to the door to see. They found that the servant had neglected to put the blood upon the posts. There the child was exposed until they found the blood and put it upon the door-posts, and when she saw it she was satisfied. That was all the assurance that she needed. So a great many are saying, "Do you feel this and that? Do you feel, do you feel, do you feel?" God does not tell you to feel. He tells you to believe. He says, "When I see the blood I will pass over," and if you are sheltered behind the blood you are perfectly safe and secure. Suppose I say to a man, "Do you feel that you own this piece of land?" He looks at me a moment and thinks I must be crazy. He says "Feel? Why feeling has nothing to do with it. I look at the title. That is all I want." So you see, all you have to do is with the title. A great many are all the time saying: "Do you feel that you are safe?" But to all God says, "He that believeth in the Lord hath everlasting life." Not "will have," it is the present tense, hath it to-day, hath it this very hour. If the devil can make you believe you will be saved sometime, and keep you from believing now and receiving now, that is all he wants. He knows that to-morrow will never come, and he puts it off from day to day, from month to month, and from year to year. My friends, Jesus Christ will never be more willing to save you than he is to-night, and the longer you put it off, the longer you wait, the further you are going from Him. Every day you put it off you are going back from God, and are making it harder for you to be saved.

My next illustration is the serpent upon the pole. You sang a song to-night about it: "It is life just to look at the Crucified One." It is not to work that we are told. It is just to look. How simple! You know a fiery serpent had gone through Israel and bitten many people, and they died. And the Israelites went to Moses and said: "Entreat the Lord to take away this serpent." They did not ask for a remedy; they did not ask for the bitten ones to be allowed to recover. They could hear the groans of the dying all around. But God more than granted their prayers. God always gives us more than we ask for. He not only took away the serpent, but He said to Moses, "Make a brass serpent and put it on a pole and lift it on high, so that all who are bitten shall look and live. And it shall come to pass that when they look, they shall not die but live." How simple! A little child can look. It is so simple that the learned and the unlearned can look. You do not have to go to college to learn how to look.

You do not have to pass through a university to learn how to look. That little child there is not more than three or four years old, but it understands how to look. If a mother wants her little child to look, she simply says, "Look, my child," and that is enough. So all that the bitten Israelites had to do was to look and live; and the very moment they looked they were saved instantaneously. It was as sudden as a flash of lightning. So many people say, "I do not understand how it is so many people can be saved all at once." Well, that is Jesus' way, and that is all there is about it. "God's thoughts are not our thoughts, and God's ways are not our ways." If we had been going to save the world, we would have gone about it in a different way from God's way, I have no doubt. If we had been going to save the bitten Israelites, the last way we would probably have thought of would have been to make a brass serpent and put it upon a pole. But God works as He pleases, and we must learn that His ways are His own and must prevail; and we must listen to Him, and if He says we will be saved at once, and that salvation is instantaneous, all we have to do is to submit and believe. Instead of looking at yourself, at your own sin, instead of looking at your past life, what you should do is just to take your eyes off of yourself and look at Christ.

Now come back again to another Bible illustration. You know when the children of Israel came from the land of slavery and had the visitation of the fiery serpents, and after Moses had been commanded to raise the brazen serpent, he went to Pisgah and died.

and Joshua led them into the Promised Land. Joshua then received a command from God that he should erect six cities, three on each side of the Jordan, which were to be cities of refuge. These places were to be put far enough apart so as to cover the whole land, that any man, no matter where he might be when he should have occasion to seek them, could easily gain access to one of them. The gates of these cities were to be kept open day and night, and the chief men of each city—the magistrates—were to keep the ways to these places free of all obstacles and stumbling-blocks, so that no one should be hindered in getting within the walls. And not only should the roads be kept smooth and well in repair, but all the bridges leading over streams and rivers should be kept up and in good condition, and sign posts were also to be placed at intervals along the road, showing the fugitive that he was on the right way—to keep him from straying. And to provide for the contingency of the man who was fleeing, not being able to read, there was a red finger put on the posts, which pointed the way. Thus a man even if he could read, was not compelled to stop and thus lose time; he saw the sign and sped on. The cities were also placed on hills, that every one could see them. The cities were erected for this purpose. It was considered a great dishonor among the Israelites if, when a man was killed, the nearest relation of him did not at once arm himself, seek out the slayer and kill him. Thus a man had no hope, if he had accidentally killed one, of saving his own life from the avenging hand of the brother or other relative, but to get within the walls of the nearest city of refuge; for it was the law that the moment he escaped that far the relation of the slain man could not touch him. Now for my illustration: Suppose I had killed a man unwittingly—that he and I had been out chopping in the woods, and suppose my axe had slipped out of my hand and had crushed in the skull of my companion. My only hope would be to get to one of these cities—my only hope was to escape for my life. I should have had no time to loiter, no time to hesitate or argue, no time to consider. I should have to start at once. The brother of my companion who had been killed, though thus purely through accident, was near and he was so incensed, or perhaps had some old score to pay off, that I should have no chance to stay and plead with him. He had made up his mind to kill me, and there was nothing left for me to do but fly. I know the young man's hot temper, and I see him on my track. I therefore spring out of the bush into the road, and it now becomes a life and death struggle. I see the city before me. Along the road I speed to the full extent of my strength. Down the hill I go as fast as I can; up the ravine I make my way; men see me coming; they do not check me, or throw any obstacles in my path; they get out of my way, and as I pass they wish me "God-speed," and warn me that the avenger is not far behind. Now I am in full view of the city; the gates are wide open; I know I shall not have to stop and knock when I get up to them. When I get closer, I see the citizens are on the walls. The information has reached them that a poor refugee is coming. Some of them have had to flee themselves, and they sympathize with me. They thus await me; but they see I am hard pressed. I am almost on the point of giving out. But I say to myself, "Courage! another effort and I shall reach the gates and be safe." Oh, if I can only reach the city! Ah, my friends, just look at the city; don't let anything take your attention away. Look! look! see what I have to do. If I stop, loiter, or linger, I am lost. The avenger will soon be on me. I can almost hear him breathing behind me. I know his sword is ready to hew me down. I get nearer to the walls now. I see the people plainly; they beckon on with their hands. I strain every nerve. "Hurry, hurry, he is almost upon you—oh, he will be killed." I bring every muscle into play. The people crowd around the gate to receive me. "Now, now," they cry. I make one more bound; I pass them; I am safe. That is instantaneous, isn't it! One minute I am under the avenging sword ready to fall upon my head; the next minute I am perfectly secure. The avenger cannot enter. The officers see to that; they will not let him come in with his sword. Can you, my friends, have a better illustration of this life? Don't you know that death is on your track now, and is ready to have you a victim? Don't you know that he may be only a few years, a few months, a few weeks, a few days, or even a few moments only, from you? Even this very afternoon he may catch up to you. You may think him miles and miles behind you, years and years away, but just as surely as you live here he is only a little way behind you now—a great deal nearer than you imagine. Haste then to a place of refuge. If you are outside the city you perish; if you come within the walls of salvation you live secure. God has a city of refuge for you. He shows you by every unmistakable sign where it is, and He gives you warning that if you do not reach its walls you die. Come then. If you neglect these mercies how do you expect to save your life? How can you loiter and linger when death is bearing down upon you? A little while and you will be lost; but if you make for the salvation offered to you, you will be safe in Christ, and you can look back and challenge death to his face. You can say in triumph, "Death, where is thy sting—grave where is thy victory."

OUT OF THE MIRE,

many a family has been raised by the genuine philanthropy of modern progress and of modern opportunities. But many people do not avail of them. They jog along in their old ways until they are stuck fast in a mire of hopeless dirt. Friends desert them, for they have already deserted themselves by neglecting their own best interests. Out of the dirt of kitchen, or hall, or parlor, any house can be quickly brought by the use of Sapolio, which is sold by all grocers.

HUGH CONWAY'S WORKS.

A Cardinal Sin.
Called Back.
Dark Days.
Slings and Arrows.
The Story of a Sculptor.
A Family Affair.
Circumstantial Evidence.
The Missing Will.

A Mental Struggle.   By The Duchess.
A False Vow.
A Broken Heart.
A Midnight Marriage.   By Holmes.
Woman against Woman.   By Holmes.
A Woman's Vengeance.   By Holmes.
A Wife's Honor.
Hilda's Lover.
Married in Haste.
At War with Herself.
A Crimson Stain.
Only a Woman's Heart.
Adventures of a Bashful Irishman.
Blunders of a Bashful Man.
One Thousand Popular Quotations.
Popular Prose Reading.
Billy's Mother.
Railroad Fun.
A Bad Boy Abroad.
The Bad Boy at Home.
Miss Slimmen's Window.
Josh Billings' Spice Box.
Vice Versa.
Phunny Phellow's Grab Bag.

J. S. OGILVIE & CO., Publishers,
31 Rose Street. New York.

THREE SPLENDID BOOKS!

THOMAS CARLYLE.
A History of the First Forty Years of His Life—1795 to 1835.
By JAMES ANTHONY FROUDE, M. A.

Two volumes in one. Price, $1.   A handsome 12mo of about 700 pages, printed from clear, handsome type, and neatly bound in English silk cloth.

This book must always be the rarest and most valuable in biographical literature—the life of one of the really dominant personalties of an epoch, written by a skillful and fearless hand, under circumstances which give it the value of autobiography, and while the personal as well as the literary influence of its subject is still potent. If the opinion of a high authority is well founded, this book will give to coming students such a faithful and vivid personal picture as has never accompanied a great name before.

FROM FARM BOY TO SENATOR.
By HORATIO ALGER, Jr.

16mo, 310 pages. Handsomely bound in cloth. Price, $1.25.

This is one of the most popular books of the present day, being a boy's life of the great American Statesman and Orator, Daniel Webster. No better book has ever been issued to put in the hands of boys. Sold by all booksellers. This book has been pronounced the best work ever written by this prince of juvenile writers. It should be in every library, and owned by every family.

NANCY HARTSHORN
At
CHAUTAUQUA.
By Mrs. NANCY HARTSHORN.

16mo, 213 pages. Illustrated. Paper cover, 50 cents; bound in cloth, $1.00.

Dedicated to all members of the Chautauqua Literary Scientific Circle, and all others who enjoy the humorous side of life.

Every one will be interested in the delineation of character as applied to "Dr. Vinson," "Mr. Beerd," "The Jubilee Singers," and others who have been there. It has been pronounced the most humorous book of the present day.

The above books are for sale by all booksellers, or will be mailed to any address on receipt of price.

THE ALBUM WRITERS FRIEND

Compiled by J. S. OGILVIE.

Paper Cover, Fifteen Cents.   Cloth, Thirty Cents.

This is a new and choice collection of gems of Prose and Poetry, comprising nearly

THREE HUNDRED SELECTIONS.

the most of which are original and suitable for writing in Autograph Albums, Valentines, and for Birthday and Wedding Celebrations. It also contains a new and choice collection of verses suitable for Christmas and New Year Cards. This is the only collection of such verses that has been printed. The many calls for such a collection has induced us to compile this book, and we offer it feeling assured that it will not only supply a want, but that it will give entire satisfaction.

It has been issued but a few weeks, and it has already received many commendations and endorsements from individuals and the Press, as being the

BEST BOOK OF THE KIND

that has been issued. The price is very low and it deserves, as we expect will receive, a wide circulation.

It contains 64 pages, and is bound in paper cover, price 15 Cents; handsomely bound in cloth, price 30 Cents.

It is for sale by every Newsdealer and Bookseller in the United States.

SEND ALL ORDERS TO
J. S. OGILVIE & CO., Publishers,
25 Rose Street, New York.

YOUMAN'S DICTIONARY

OF

EVERY-DAY WANTS.

Containing 20,000 Receipts in Every Department of Human Effort.

BY A. E. YOUMAN, M. D.

Royal Octavo, 530 Pages. Price in Cloth, $4.00; Leather, $4.75

$100 a Year Saved to all who Possess and Read this Book!

No book of greater value was ever offered to Agents to sell. The following list of trades and professions are fully represented, and information of great value given in each department. Our 16-page circular, giving full description, sent free to any address.

Clerks,	Lumber Dealers,	Hardware Dealers,	Watchmakers,
Bookkeepers,	Miners,	Engravers,	Dyers,
Farmers,	Opticians,	Furriers,	Coopers,
Stock-raisers,	Whitewashers,	Glaziers,	Coppersmiths,
Gardeners,	Soapmakers,	Grocers,	Machinists,
Florists,	Trappers,	Hotel Keepers,	Curriers,
Builders,	Tinsmiths,	Iron Workers,	Doctors,
Merchants,	Cabinetmakers,	Authors,	Egg Dealers,
Druggists,	Housekeepers,	Nurses,	Electrotypers,
Photographers,	Bankers,	Perfumers,	Fish Dealers,
Architects,	Barbers,	Roofers,	Gas Burners,
Artists,	Inspectors,	Stereotypers,	Glove Cleaners,
Bakers,	Bookbinders,	Tanners,	Gunsmiths,
Confectioners,	Gilders,	Varnishers,	Hucksters,
Engineers,	Painters,	Cooks,	Lithographers,
Flour Dealers,	Shoemakers,	Builders,	Milliners,
Glass Workers,	Clothiers,	Dairymen,	Dentists,
Hair Dressers,	Dressmakers,	Carpenters,	Plasterers,
Hatters,	Dry Goods Dealers,	Carvers,	Scourers,
Ink Makers,	Brewers,	Jewelers,	Tailors,

We want Agents everywhere to sell this invaluable work, to whom we offer big pay. A copy of the book will be sent by mail, postpaid, to any address, upon receipt of price. For agents' terms, territory, and further particulars, address

J. S. OGILVIE & CO., Publishers,

P. O. Box 2767, 31 ROSE STREET, New York.

HUMOROUS BOOKS.

*"A little nonsense now and then
Is relished by the wisest men."*

The following list of books have been written and published with a view to give the mind the relaxation which every person needs and should have. Read these books and you will find that they will lighten the load on your mind, and "drive dull care away." They are all written by well known and popular authors.

A Bad Boy's Diary. This is one of the most successful humorous books of the present day, filled with fun and good humor, and "will drive the blues out of a bag of indigo." 12mo, 280 pages. Handsomely lithographed paper cover, printed in four colors, 50 cents; cloth, with handsome gold side-stamp, $1.00.

The Blunders of a Bashful Man. By the popular author of "A Bad Boy's Diary." This is one of the most humorous books ever issued. 12mo, 160 pages. Handsomely illustrated from original designs, including also the portrait and autograph of "The Bashful Man." Price, paper cover, 25 cents; handsomely bound in cloth, 60 cents.

A Bushel of Fun. Gathered from the writings of the leading and most successful humorists of the day. Price, 10 cts.

Chained Lightning. By "Ike Philkins," one of the most noted funny men of the age. A whole volume of Jolly Jokes, Quaint Anecdotes, Funny Stories, and Brilliant Witticisms. 12mo, 104 pages. Price, 25 cents.

Diary of a Minister's Wife. By Almedia M. Brown. 12mo, 544 pages. Handsomely bound in cloth, with fine, full-page illustrations. Price, $1.50.

Diary of a Village Gossip. By Almedia M. Brown. 12mo, 293 pages. Paper cover, 50 cents; handsomely bound in cloth, $1.00.

Ha! Ha! Ha! or, Morsels of Mirth for Funny Fellows. We warrant this book to be a sure cure for every ailment under and above the moon, sun, stars, and comets. 64 pages. Price, 10 cts.

Josh Billings' Spice Box. Edited by Josh Billings himself, and dedicated to all who love fun. It contains 64 large quarto pages and nearly 200 illustrations, any one of which will cause a broad grin on anyone's face. Price, 25 cents.

The above books are for sale by all newsdealers and booksellers, or will be mailed to any address, postpaid, on receipt of price. Address all orders to

J. S. OGILVIE & CO. Publishers,

P. O. Box 2767. 31 Rose Street New York.

Something to Read!

$10.00 WORTH FOR $1.50!

We desire to call the attention of lovers of pure fiction to the fact that we now offer, in *bound book form*, the following seven complete stories, written by

Mrs. Henry Wood,

one of the most popular and pleasing authors in the world, and which are usually sold, in book form, for from $1.25 to $1.50 EACH.

We offer the SEVEN STORIES, bound in handsome English cloth, with elegant ornamental gold side and back stamp, sent by mail, post-paid, to any address, for only $1.50! Bound in heavy paper covers, $1.00.

List of Stories we send for $1.50:

East Lynne;
A Life's Secret;
The Tale of Sin;
Was He Severe?
The Lost Bank-Note;
The Doctor's Daughter;
The Haunted Tower.

These stories are printed on fine heavy paper, from large, new type, and we guarantee satisfaction in *every respect* to all purchasers.

Ask your bookseller for "SOMETHING TO READ," published by us; or send $1.50 to us and we will send them by mail, post-paid.

THE STORIES ARE NOT SOLD SEPARATELY IN THIS FORM. We want Agents to sell them in every town and village in the whole land, to whom we offer liberal terms.

Address all orders and applications for Agency to

J. S. OGILVIE & CO., Publishers,

P. O. Box 2767.   25 Rose Street, New York.

Something to Read!

$10.00 WORTH FOR $1.50!

We desire to call the attention of lovers of pure fiction to the fact that we now offer, in *bound book form*, the following seven complete stories, written by

Miss M. E. Braddon,

one of the most popular and pleasing authors in the world, and which are usually sold, in book form, for from $1.25 to $1.50 EACH.

We offer the SEVEN STORIES, bound in handsome English cloth, with elegant ornamental gold side and back stamp, sent by mail, post-paid, to any address, for only $1.50! Bound in heavy paper covers, $1.00.

List of Stories we sell for $1.50:

Lady Audley's Secret
The Octoroon,
The Cloven Foot,
His Secret,
A Wavering Image,
The Wages of Sin,
Aurora Floyd.

These stories are printed on fine heavy paper, from large, new type, and we guarantee satisfaction in *every respect* to all purchasers.

Ask your bookseller for "SOMETHING TO READ," written by Miss M. E. Braddon, and published by us; or send $1.50 to us and we will send them by mail, post paid.

THE STORIES ARE NOT SOLD SEPARATELY IN THIS FORM. We want Agents to sell them in every town and village in the whole land, to whom we offer liberal terms.

Address all orders and applications for Agency to

J. S. OGILVIE & CO., Publishers,

P. O. Box 2767,   25 Rose Street, New York.

Two Grand Detective Stories

BY

JUDSON R. TAYLOR,

One of the most popular writers in the world.

GIPSY BLAIR,
THE WESTERN DETECTIVE.

12mo, 150 pages, paper cover, 25 cents; handsomely bound in cloth, 60 cents.

This is one of the most thrilling detective stories ever written by this well-known and popular writer, and relates deeds of daring adventure, and consummate detective skill in tracing the violators of law. Every one should read it, because it is a story of intense interest and dramatic power.

MACON MOORE,
THE SOUTHERN DETECTIVE.

12mo, 150 pages, paper cover, 25 cents; handsomely bound in cloth, 60 cents.

This is truly a most wonderful story, with the above title, and is probably the most extraordinary detective story ever written. The author has used his abundance of material very skillfully, and although the incidents are mainly founded on fact, they are so deftly linked together as to form a romance at once grand, terrible, and startling. As a thrilling detective story, it would be impossible to surpass it. In fact, there is nothing in the English language like it. In fact, taken altogether, the story is the most extraordinary detective romance ever given to the world, and all who fail to read it will miss a rich treat. Both of the above books are sold by all booksellers, or they will be mailed to any address on receipt of price.

Address all orders to

J. S. OGILVIE & CO., Publishers,

P. O. Box 2767. 31 Rose Street, New York.

HUGH CONWAY'S POPULAR WORKS,

Price, in Paper Cover, 25 Cents Each.

CALLED BACK.

By Hugh Conway.

This novel has met with an unprecedented sale, and is pronounced one of the ablest written books ever issued. It is full of interest, and entrances all readers.

The Pall Mall Gazette says of it:

"Called Back" is entitled to, and will doubtless take its place in the front rank of pure fiction. The sale of over 200,000 copies already is some indication of its well-deserved popularity.

DARK DAYS.

This new novel by Hugh Conway, the now famous author, is now ready, and from advance orders already received an immense sale is assured for it. No book has been issued for years, the announcement of which has created such an intense interest as this has.

It has about 200 pages in large type. Price, paper cover, 25 cents.

THE MISSING WILL.

Another popular novel by this great author; 12mo, 175 pages. Paper cover, 25 cents.

CIRCUMSTANTIAL EVIDENCE,

AND OTHER STORIES.

This is the latest collection of stories by Hugh Conway, and will be eagerly sought after by all who have read his other works. 12mo, 180 pages. Paper cover, 25 cents.

Sent by mail, post-paid, to any address, on receipt of price. Address all orders to

J. S. OGILVIE & CO., Publishers,

P. O. Box 2767.   31 Rose St., NEW YORK.

A $10.00 BOOK FOR $2.50!

MOORE'S
UNIVERSAL ASSISTANT AND COMPLETE MECHANIC,

Containing over One Million Industrial Facts,

CALCULATIONS, PROCESSES, TRADE SECRETS, RULES, LEGAL ITEMS, BUSINESS FORMS, etc., in every Occupation, from the Household to the Manufactory.

A work of unequaled utility to every Mechanic, Farmer, Merchant, Business Man, Professional Gentleman, and Householder, as it embraces the main points in over 200 Trades and Occupations. It contains 1016 pages and over 500 illustrations.

The following synopsis gives some idea of the value and scope of the work. The contents are as follows:

Part 1.—Bread, Cracker, Pastry and Cake Baking, Domestic Cooking, etc.
Part 2.—For Farmers, Horse Shoers, Stock Owners, Bee Keepers, etc.
Part 3.—For Lumbermen, Carpenters, Builders, Contractors, Mill Owners, Shipbuilders, Ship Owners, Freighters, Navigators, Quarrymen, Merchants and Business Men generally.
Part 4.—Natural Mechanical and Scientific Facts.
Part 5.—For Dyers, Clothiers, Bleachers, Hatters, Furriers and Manufacturers.
Art 6.—Medical Department, for Druggists, Physicians, Dentists, Perfumers, Barbers, and general Family Use.
Part 7.—For Grocers, Tobacconists, Confectioners, Saloon Keepers, Syrups, Cordials, Ice Creams, Summer Drinks, Domestic Wines, Canned Goods, Soaps, etc.
Part 8.—For Tanners and Curriers, Boot, Shoe, Harness and Rubber Manufacturers, Marble and Ivory Workers, Bookbinders, Anglers, Trappers, etc.
Part 9.—For Painters, Decorators, Cabinet Makers, Piano and Organ Manufacturers, Polishers, Carvers, Gilders, Picture Frame and Art Dealers, China Decorators, Potters, Glass Manufacturers, Glass Stainers and Gilders, Architects, Masons, Bricklayers, Plasterers, Stucco Workers, Kalsominers, Slaters, Roofers, etc.
Part 10.—For Watchmakers, Jewelers, Gold and Silversmiths, Gilders, Burnishers, Colorers, Enamelers, Lapidaries, Diamond Cutters, Engravers, Die Sinkers, Stencil Cutters, Refiners, Sweepmelters.
Part 11.—For Engineers, Firemen, Engine Builders, Steam Fitters, Master Mechanics, Machinists, Blacksmiths, Cutlers, Locksmiths, Saw, Spring, and Safe Manufacturers, Iron and Brass Founders, Mill Owners, Miners, etc.
Part 12.—For Art Workers, Bronzing, Dipping and Lacquering, Brass Finishers, Hardware Dealers, Plumbers, Gas Fitters, Tinman, Japanners, etc.
Part 13.—For Printers and Publishers, Gas Companies and Consumers, Gunsmiths, Contractors, Quarrymen, Coal Dealers, Oil Manufacturers, Sugar Refiners, Paper Manufacturers, Cotton and Woolen Manufacturers, Cutlers, Needle and File Manufacturers, Metal Smelters, etc., etc.
Part 14.—The Amenities of Life, Useful Advice.
Part 15.—Tables, etc., Embracing Useful Calculations in every Business.

Price in Cloth Binding, $2.50; in Leather Binding, $3.50. Standard Export Edition, Cloth Binding, $3.00; in Leather, Lettered Back and Marbled Edges, Library Style, $4.00.

Sent by mail, postpaid, to any address on receipt of price. Agents wanted, to whom we offer big pay. Address all orders and applications for an agency to

J. S. OGILVIE & CO., Publishers,

P. O Box 2767. 31 Rose Street, New York

www.ingramcontent.com/pod-product-compliance
Lightning Source LLC
Chambersburg PA
CBHW032137160426
43197CB00008B/683